# *from* FORBIDDEN
# *to* FOREVER

# An unconventional love story.

*By Kris Calbar*

ISBN-10: 0692928952
ISBN-13: 978-0692928950 (Zenbar Books)

# DEDICATION

*My dearest Wayne,*

*Of all the lifetimes we have shared, this one is by far my favorite.*
*I love you most forevermore.*
*xoxo*

# CONTENTS

# ACKNOWLEDGMENTS

Special thanks to my beloved Wayne for creating the cover for this book and for his tireless support of my writing endeavors.

I'd also like to thank Janet and especially Lorena for giving me more material to write about. Without you, this book would have been much shorter and far less entertaining.

More appreciation goes out to my parents and in-laws for their unconditional love and support.

Last but not least, I'd like to thank our amazing kids, Lea and Sebastian, for being such an integral part of this beautifully blended family and our little bird, Phoenix, for helping us rise even higher from the ashes.

# PROLOGUE

I blame it on his firework smile and the way it crinkles the corners of his beautiful brown eyes. He fired one sunshine smile at me and I was instantly and irreparably blinded to any potential future that did not have him on center stage in the play that is my life.

My mind was quick to protest. A man? Surely there must be some sort of mistake. Fate was notorious for casting only female leads and yet there he was, the newest and most prominent character my life had ever known, proposing drastic revisions to my story with all of his masculine glory. Resistance was futile. Our first kiss only served to convince my mind of what my heart already suspected: no other script but his would ever be enough.

Fear tried to sneak its way into the picture followed soon after by doubt. We were both in the tail end of failing marriages involving children. Despite mutual unhappiness on both ends, we were still attached to other people and there were a lot of strings that would need to be cut in order for us to begin a relationship of our own. Nothing about it would be quick or simple. The horizon was littered with drama and emotional land mines as far as the eyes could see and it was hard to imagine how any relationship could withstand so many obstacles, particularly one so shiny and new.

Well I am happy to report that our relationship was clearly built to last because to date it has withstood the fiercest of storms and somehow still floats happily along the horizon of ever after without so much as a battle scar to speak of. Often while cuddled up close before drifting off to sleep in each other's arms, we reminisce on the crazy series of events that led us to the current moment and marvel at this force field of love, more powerful than anything either of us has ever known.

Ours is not your average love story. I feel compelled to share it with the world because despite the inevitable backlash from holier-than-thou types who will harshly judge many of the difficult decisions we made along the way or the LGBT community that may disapprove of my newfound love for a member of the opposite sex, our story is proof that there is no better GPS than the human heart.

Pack an open mind and heart as you join me on this special journey. The pages that follow will retrace the steps that led me to true love's door and dared my heart to knock like never before. Stepping over the threshold of that door was both the most terrifying and the best decision I have ever made.

# CHAPTER 1: COLLISION COURSE

I was married to a woman. Though we had conducted a small, informal ceremony early in the relationship, she and I had been together for about 8 years before we made the marriage legally official (mostly because it wasn't legally permitted until then). The relationship with my wife, Janet, at the time and for quite some time before then was no walk in the park. I realize that every relationship has its ups and its downs but if I were to diagram the full length of our relationship from beginning to end, there would be far more valleys than hills in even my most generous rendition of it. The truth is that we were doomed from early on due to a major disconnect on every imaginable level and a lack of equal enthusiasm to try and change that. I did everything I could think of to regain our initial connection and increase intimacy between us but she resisted every effort for years on end. I vocalized my disappointment and frustrations to her on multiple occasions but my cries fell on deaf ears. It was not until she realized I had given up that she began to show any interest in saving the relationship but by that time it was far too late.

Prior to meeting the man who had changed it all, I had resigned myself to a life of unhappiness with Janet. I had considered leaving the relationship before we were legally married and openly shared my doubts about marriage with her but she always convinced me that things were "not that bad" and would get better. I resented that her expectations for our relationship seemed to be satisfied by falling short of terrible. I wanted a relationship that was happy and healthy, not one that was merely tolerable. She put a lot of pressure on me to get married and despite some initial resistance; I eventually started to believe that things might get better if I gave her what she wanted. After all, I reasoned, I had already invested a great deal of time in the relationship and we had a child together so it seemed like a logical step to take at that moment. It didn't take long after our marriage was officially legal, though, for me to realize what a tremendous mistake I had made. I was newly married to someone I had known and loved for many years and someone I had built a family with and yet I never felt more alone. We were together all the time but there was no connection anymore. We rarely kissed or touched each other and even when we did it felt awkward and forced. Making love to her had long felt more like a dreaded chore than an enjoyable way to deepen intimacy. It had been years since sex with her had any effect beyond reminding me of how disconnected we were.

I was frustrated on every level and that frustration was further aggravating my already compromised relationship. By that point I had been logging our sex life, or lack thereof, for some time. I kept a detailed record of each time I had attempted to initiate any type of romantic or sexual connection between us and been rejected. The harshest entries, though, were the ones where my attempts were successful and the result was an even bigger disappointment than the rejection. She was completely uninterested in me romantically and it was painfully obvious with every touch.

I began to resent my wife. Every little thing she said or did would irritate me. Our relationship started to fluctuate between periods of intense fighting to periods of complete disconnection and indifference until the only happy moments left were those in my long lost memories of our early days. There was a great deal of anger and hostility between us. Close friends and family members who we used to spend a lot of time with grew distant because the palpable tension that we seemed to radiate was too uncomfortable for them to handle. We were most uncomfortable. Janet, our toddler, and I were all simply existing in a seemingly endless stream of unhappiness and dissatisfaction yet we kept pretending things were "not that bad" for far longer than we should have.

At only two years old, our daughter, Lea, was too young to understand what was happening but I knew that she could sense the tension just as much as we could. At first I thought that I owed it to Lea to stay and try to make things work but the worse things got, the more I realized that I had it backwards. I owed it to Lea to end what was clearly an unhealthy relationship and show her that life is too short to settle in love or in anything else. That realization came a long time later, though. Truth is, I should have left the moment that I realized we were no longer compatible but it took me a long, long time to be able to admit that and even longer to actually do something about it. On the other hand, perhaps it was just the right amount of time. I do tend to believe that things happen as and when they should. Maybe we both needed to endure those last rocky years together in order to learn the lessons that we might not have been able to understand under different circumstances. Or maybe, just maybe, walking that treacherous winding road was the only way that my path would ever intersect with the path of the man my heart was unknowingly destined for. Perhaps that is why fate kept urging both him and me along such hostile terrain, inching us closer and closer to each other.

Have you ever felt compelled to do something seemingly irrational but the idea continued to haunt you despite its lack of sense? I can't tell you the precise moment when it happened but it was as if I woke up on what should have been an average day and felt like the universe itself was yanking on my invisible puppet strings, moving me closer towards what would ultimately become a new destiny. Initially I tried to dismiss the thought as nothing short of unreasonable and downright dangerous, but it was almost like the idea had a mind of its own and was refusing to take "no" for an answer. It was an inexplicable urge to post a personals ad on the infamous Craigslist website looking for meaningless sex with none other than a male stranger. I literally laughed out loud at this notion on more than one occasion. Was I having some sort of premature midlife crisis? It was ludicrous on so many levels and yet the idea had burrowed itself so deeply into my mind that it became more and more difficult to ignore, the urge growing in intensity with each passing day.

I wasn't living under a rock. I was well aware of the inherent dangers associated with any type of interaction with strangers on Craigslist and understood that openly seeking a sexual encounter on there would undoubtedly attract an obscene amount of creeps and crazies, but somehow even that knowledge was incapable of quieting this curious new urge of mine. Never mind the fact that I had identified as a lesbian for all of my adult life or recently married the woman I had been romantically involved with for nearly the last decade and was raising a child with. I had every reason in the world to reject this ridiculous urge but the more I resisted, the stronger it grew until my every thought was consumed by it. Eventually I surrendered to the possibility that the only way to truly quiet the urge would be to indulge it, no matter how ludicrous.

As I stumbled along my broken path, torn between indulging my crazy urge or just walking away from Janet and starting over again altogether, my twin flame, Wayne, had just gotten his first peek at greener pastures along the dark and dreary path he had been walking on his end. Before we met, Wayne was unhappily married for pretty much the entire duration of the eleven or so years that he and his wife, Lorena had been together. Despite having convinced him that she was on birth control, Lorena became pregnant within a month of them dating. He later found out that she also had a young daughter from a previous relationship. Lorena didn't have much of a motherly instinct, though, as she left the bulk of parenting to the maternal grandmother so that she could be free to do as she pleased without the pesky responsibilities of being a mother weighing her down. While he had no shortage of reservations about Lorena, Wayne married her out of a sense of responsibility to his unborn child.

Wayne and Lorena's marriage was a rocky one from the start. I suppose that is how it goes when two people get married because they feel like they should rather than because they truly want to, not unlike what had happened between Janet and me. The years passed and Wayne stuck around for the sake of his son, Sebastian. He found creative ways to endure his unhappy marriage by keeping his life as separate as possible from Lorena's. They were legally married on paper but their day-to-day lives were completely disconnected. By the time Wayne and I met, he and Lorena were more like roommates with an occasional sex life than anything else. They had separate bank accounts and even separate households. Lorena financially maintained her mother's house and spent the majority of her time there. She kept her personal things at her mother's house and showered there daily. Lorena was essentially a part-time resident at the home where Wayne lived. She basically only slept there, sharing the bed with Wayne and their pre-teen, Sebastian, who occupied the space between them.

Wayne and Lorena had a weekly dinner date, which I suppose was her way of trying to remind him that he had a wife because every other day, he openly urged her to stay away for as long as possible. Despite this odd arrangement that they had, Wayne somehow remained faithful to her for all of those years. He, like me, had resigned himself to a lifetime sentence within an unhappy marriage.

May of 2015 was an important month for both Wayne and me. For him, it was the month that he left Lorena behind to join his sister and some friends on a trip to Italy. Thanks to some ongoing legal troubles, Lorena was unable to leave the country so Wayne decided to take the opportunity to go for himself. It was the first time in more than a decade that he had traveled anywhere without her and the experience turned out to be a pivotal turning point for him. While in Italy, Wayne realized how much happier he was without Lorena dragging him down. Something shifted in him and he decided that he wanted things to change, though he was not sure at the time exactly what that change would look like for him. Thousands of miles away around the same time, I was going through a metamorphosis of my own. After one of the many disappointing sexual encounters with Janet, something shifted in me too. I was tired of feeling inadequate and unworthy of love or affection. I was finally ready to indulge my mysterious urge in the hopes that I might be able to get at least one of my unmet needs satisfied.

I posted a personals ad in the casual encounters section of Craigslist. While I can't recall exactly what my ad said, it was something along the lines of a married but lonely, plus-size woman seeking no strings attached and drama free sex with a healthy and sane stranger, preferably one who was also married. I realize how unethical this was. Looking to cheat was bad enough but specifically seeking somebody who was also cheating made it worse, I know. In my mind, it was safer for me to take a risk with somebody who had as much to lose as I did. Also, I thought it would make it easier to keep things casual that way since both of us would be invested elsewhere. It might be confusing to some that a woman in a lesbian relationship who was looking to cheat would seek a man rather than a woman but in my mind it was the only reasonable choice. Choosing a man made sense to me because I had always been physically attracted to men, but romantic relationships with men had never appealed to me. I genuinely believed that I was incapable of falling in love with a man because in my thirty something years of life, I had only fallen in love with women. Wayne was not the first man I had experienced sexually. I had been with men before Wayne but my interest in them never seemed to go beyond temporary playthings. Until Wayne came into my life, I had never met a man who didn't annoy or bore me within a few days of meeting him so I thought a man was the perfect specimen for the meaningless sex that I decided was necessary at that point in my life.

As you can probably imagine, there was no shortage of colorful responses to my ad. I wasn't expecting such an avalanche of interest but that's precisely what I got and it was rather overwhelming at first. As I sifted through hundreds of replies ranging from one-word messages to a series of unsolicited penis pictures and everything in between, I questioned my sanity more than a handful of times. Nevertheless something urged me to keep sifting. I responded to most of the replies that sounded relatively normal and exchanged a series of messages with a few of them. I felt like I was searching for a needle in a haystack but I had no idea why, what the needle looked like, or if I was even in the right haystack.

Using Craigslist to search for casual sex with a man felt really awkward the entire time and I kept second-guessing what the hell I was doing. I posted a total of 3 ads. I left the first one up for only a few hours and then deleted it to give myself a chance to weed through the responses and see if I could find some sense in what I was doing but I still lacked any real direction. I realize how ridiculous it sounds but I thought that maybe if I found a clean and decent guy to have sex with, then perhaps my urge would quiet down and I could get on with my unhappy marriage in somewhat better spirits. I was genuinely surprised to find such high numbers of men in what seemed to be similar situations. So many people unsatisfied within their marriages for one reason or another. It was truly a rather sad realization and continues to be an unfortunate reality for far too many people. Life is too short for so many people to be living lives that leave them unfulfilled with people they aren't truly happy to share them with.

I posted a second ad a day or two later and went through the same process. That time around there was one guy who stood out from the rest. Eddie was funny and I enjoyed talking to him. There was a sort of chemistry in our conversations and I was curious to see if that might carry over to a real life meeting but at the same time I wanted to be extra cautious. I wasn't interested in ruining my family or his and besides, I was still wary of the fact that we met over Craigslist and he could potentially be somebody dangerous. We each talked about our situations and what brought us to where we were at that point in our lives. I told Eddie how important it was for me to find somebody that I could trust. I made it clear that aside from discretion and full disclosure about health status, my number one priority for moving forward with continuing to get to know each other and potentially meet was that we both agree to be completely honest with each other about everything.

I was not interested in juggling multiple friends with benefits and did not want to be sexually involved with someone who was being too promiscuous either. I realize how ridiculous that may seem. Obviously by nature of the circumstances under which we met, there was already a clear precedence for betrayal and dishonesty but somehow I wasn't convinced that every Craigslist creeper was irreparably bankrupt on a moral level. I also realize that I was not exactly engaging in very righteous behavior either and I was not trying to judge anybody for their decisions or actions but if I was going to allow myself to be intimate with somebody new, I wanted to minimize the risk for any surprises on either end.

Eddie claimed to be on the same page as me so after a few days of exchanging messages and pictures, I decided to go ahead and set up a meeting in a public place. We met during daytime hours underneath a pavilion at a nearby park and had a brief, awkward conversation while sitting across from each other at a picnic table. We talked about our families and how crazy it was to be doing what we were doing. The chemistry we seemed to have during our email exchange was replaced by jittery nerves and a palpable weirdness. It was uncomfortable and after about ten minutes, I told him that I had to go. Eddie insisted on walking me to my car and told me that he would email me later. I held out my hand to give him a handshake but he pulled me in and kissed me instead. The kiss caught me off guard but it was mostly unremarkable. I headed home, unsure of whether or not I was interested in seeing him again. It was hard for me to tell if I was just too nervous or if there was something about Eddie that I didn't like.

Eddie emailed me within the hour trying to make plans for another meeting. I felt like something was off about him. I wasn't sure what it was but he came off as if he made a habit of this sort of thing even though I had directly asked him and he insisted it was new to him and that he was looking for the same thing as me. I didn't believe him so I checked the casual encounters section for ads posted by men and found a number of solicitations that were likely to be him. He had a unique eloquence to him that most people trolling on Craigslist seemed to lack, which is mostly what drew me to him in the first place. Most of the posts were a month or older but one posted minutes earlier caught my attention. If it was him, he emailed me asking to move forward to a second meeting and then almost immediately afterwards posted a new ad looking for another partner in crime. I replied anonymously to the ad and requested a picture. It didn't take long to receive a fresh copy of his mug in my inbox along with the beginning of a dialogue that had a very familiar ring to it. I humored him a bit, exchanging a few emails and confirming my suspicion that this guy was a Craigslist whore looking to add as many conquests as possible to his collection. I certainly never wanted any claim to Eddie and had no issues with him collecting women to his heart's content if that's what he wanted to do. My issue was that I expected him to be honest with me about what he was doing so that I could then make an informed decision about whether or not I wanted to be one of those women. Obviously it was silly of me to assume that he could be honest with someone like me when he was clearly so comfortable sleeping around on his wife. I was frustrated that I allowed myself to believe that there could be such a thing as an "honest" adulterous man. What in the world was I thinking?!? The sheer lunacy of these ideas made no sense even to me as they danced around in my own mind.

Later that night, I replied to Eddie's email about meeting a second time and told him that I was not interested in seeing him again. He insisted on me giving him a reason so I told him that I was one of the women who had replied to his new ad. Eddie became immediately enraged and defensive. We exchanged a few heated emails and then I decided to mark him as spam and end the conversation for good. I had enough drama in my life with a perpetually angry wife so I certainly did not need it from some strange guy that I didn't even know or care to.

The entire experience with Eddie had left a bad taste in my mouth so I told myself to stop with the Craigslist nonsense and move on with my life. I put it all out of my head for a couple of days but that damn urge kept popping up despite my best efforts to ignore it. I distinctly remember wondering what in the world fate could be trying to accomplish by pushing me back to the cesspool of Craigslist over and over again. I started getting frustrated and annoyed by this incessant tugging on my invisible strings. Reluctantly, I posted a third ad in casual encounters and almost immediately resented myself for doing so.

It was like I was battling the infamous angel and devil on my shoulder. My angel was sick and tired of the devil leading me down a path that I could not understand but for some reason it continued to go along with it anyway, bitching and complaining every step of the way. History seemed to repeat itself as tons of replies started pouring in within minutes of posting the ad. At this point, my attitude about the whole thing was not exactly cheerful so the few men I responded to that time around received messages that were short and to the point. I did not want to waste any time bantering back and forth with a series of strange men on the Internet.

My mission became centered on finding somebody that did not totally suck and testing out chemistry on a different but sufficiently discreet platform, like KIK.

That day I ended up starting a KIK conversation with three different guys, one of which happened to be Wayne. One of the other guys was really nice to chat with but when he admitted to me that he is on the sexual predator list for some alleged "miscommunication" with an underage girlfriend's parents, he made it to my block list pretty quickly. I got along well with Carlos, the first guy that I started chatting with on KIK, but he was in his late twenties, which was younger than my comfort level allowed so I made it clear to him that any communication between us would remain strictly platonic and would never move into the real world.

Meanwhile Wayne and I hit it off almost immediately. Our chats flowed easily and I instantly felt like I could tell him anything. I remember thinking how unusual it was that our conversation over something like text could feel so natural. I kept reminding myself not to get my hopes up about Wayne because it was likely artificial anyway and he might end up along the same lines as Eddie had. Wayne grew on me very quickly so I made a conscious effort to restrict our text time and keep my guard up as much as possible. I sensed that Wayne might make it easy for me to drop that guard and I didn't think I wanted things to go that route.

Wayne's initial email in response to my ad told me that he wanted a "part-time relationship" to help him cope with being stuck in an unhappy marriage. This message was somewhat worrisome to me because the word "relationship" implied that at least a few strings might be attached, even if it was only "part-time" and I was determined to avoid even the smallest of attachment to somebody new.

I wanted strictly no strings attached sex with a consistent partner and I genuinely believed that because I sought a man, I could easily avoid any potential for emotional or romantic interest in him beyond the bedroom. I wanted Wayne to be aware of this and did not want to waste his time or mine so about ten minutes into our first KIK conversation, I told Wayne about the issues I was having with my wife. If only I could have been a fly on the wall and seen his face when he read those words. To say that I caught him off guard would be an understatement. He was understandably confused and had many questions about whether I meant to say "wife," about whether I was aware that he was a man, and finally, if perhaps I had accidentally placed my ad in the wrong section. I was literally laughing out loud and reassured Wayne that while I did mean to say wife and I did know that he was a man, I knew exactly what section I was posting my ad in and had done so deliberately.

I went on to explain to Wayne that I was specifically seeking a man because I believed that it was the easiest way for me to remain detached and that men are essentially only organic sex toys for me.

Despite his uneasiness about my blunt description of what I was looking for, Wayne and I continued to hit it off via text and we soon established our one rule for moving forward: 100% honesty. Since we could not be honest with our wives, we were committed to being painfully honest with each other. Though I did not know much about him at that point and understood that he could potentially be lying just as Eddie had, I somehow felt like I could genuinely trust Wayne. I had no real reason to trust him and in fact had reasons not to considering the circumstances under which we met but somehow that didn't seem to matter. I trusted him wholeheartedly and that seemed to excite me as much as it scared me.

Wayne and I chatted on and off through KIK for about a week before I asked him if we could meet in person. We decided to meet at a Starbucks a couple of days later. Since we lived about 30 minutes away from each other, we chose a Starbucks that was somewhere near the halfway point and scheduled our meeting for a Friday afternoon. In preparation for my first date with Wayne, I made a list of questions that we could both answer so that we would have something to keep the conversation going through the inevitable awkwardness of a first meeting.

I got to the Starbucks a few minutes early so I was the first to arrive. I went to the far end of the store and found an empty table to sit at. I switched tables about 3 times before I finally settled on the right vantage point so that I could see Wayne clearly when he came through the front door. It was the first week of June in 2015 and I naively sat at the Starbucks table completely unaware that my life was about to take an extremely sharp turn. Wayne and I were about to collide.

# CHAPTER 2: COSMIC CONNECTIONS

Life is a series of pivotal moments that define and guide us in whatever direction may be meant for us at any given point in time. I saw it best expressed in a quote by author John Hobbes that says, "There are moments which mark your life. Moments when you realize nothing will ever be the same and time is divided into two parts, before this, and after this." I can say with unequivocal certainty that the moment Wayne walked through that Starbucks door was one mammoth pivotal moment for me and my life has been exponentially better ever since.

The image of that tall, handsome stranger walking into Starbucks is forever etched into my mind. I was worried that I might not recognize him in person since I had only seen a few pictures of him during our chats but I instantly knew it was him. Wearing jeans and a black t-shirt, he came straight for the table I was sitting at and we exchanged an awkward greeting before sitting across from each other. Both of our hands rested on the table and I wanted to grab hold of his hand but wasn't sure how he would react so I never did. To this day he complains that I didn't seem like I wanted to hold his hand that day. Neither of us ever ordered coffee. We sat across from each other, looking into each other's eyes more often than I would normally find comfortable with a stranger and sharing answers to the questions I had prepared.

Throughout the conversation I searched for any sign of a red flag but could not find any, which in a way was its own red flag. I worried that he might be too good to be true. And then I worried that he might actually be that good and that was an even scarier thought. It was clear from early on that he was no ordinary man and I knew from the moment I looked into his eyes that he was going to change my life in some significant way. After just under an hour of talking, Wayne and I walked out of the Starbucks together and hugged each other goodbye in the parking lot. The comfort of that first embrace spoke volumes. There was no awkwardness in it; only a feeling of warmth and happiness that made me not want to let him go. I had no doubts about wanting to see him again. Shortly afterwards, I sent him a message telling him how much I enjoyed meeting him and that I was looking forward to seeing him again. We made plans to meet the following week at a public park.

During the days leading up to our second date, Wayne and I continued to chat through KIK. I noticed that the amount of contact between us was gradually increasing. Normally that would have scared me off and I would have made up some excuse to disappear like I had with other potential friends with benefits before him but with Wayne, I welcomed the increased communication. I found myself smiling when I heard the KIK notifications go off and wanting to talk to him more and more. The hours before I could see him again seemed to drag. I was eager to be in his presence again and had made up my mind that I would not leave our second date without kissing him. I was excited to see him but also apprehensive about being too enthusiastic. I had to keep reminding myself that Wayne and I were both married to other people and that this arrangement was to remain strictly sexual so I should avoid attachment at all costs. I truly thought then that it would be possible to accomplish this. I reassured myself by thinking of all the other guys who I had been so physically attracted to but emotionally unimpressed by. Men were good for eye candy or a good time in bed but it never took long for them to get on my nerves or for me to get bored with them. I assumed that Wayne would end up on that list sooner rather than later. I dismissed the powerful connection I felt towards him as intense infatuation or lust. Until Wayne proved me wrong, I genuinely believed that it was not possible for me to fall in love with a man. Despite my unexpected enthusiasm over a man I had only met in person once, I convinced myself that it would soon turn to annoyance and that I was safe to proceed without serious risk of emotional attachment.

When the day of our second date finally arrived, I could hardly contain my excitement. Wayne and I planned to meet at a public park near my job for a short while in the afternoon hours. I arrived first and waited for him in the car. A few minutes later, he pulled up and parked his car next to mine. The butterflies in my stomach ran wild as I got out of my car and hopped into his passenger seat. We exchanged a nervous kiss on the cheek and awkward hellos. We were both visibly nervous and I was somewhat paranoid. There were a lot of people walking around the park and other cars parked nearby. Being so close to work and home, I worried that someone I know might pass by and see me in the car with an unknown man. The fear of Janet discovering my betrayal was powerful at that time.

After a few minutes of small talk, Wayne kissed me and the world seemed to stand still in that moment. The details from the rest of that day are a bit fuzzy. My mind was spinning in so many directions and my body responded to him as if he were some sort of magnet. I had not planned to go farther than kissing that day, particularly considering that we were in a public place, but that plan was quickly abandoned. I could not seem to keep my hands off of him or resist his hands on me.

Wayne drove around the park looking for the most secluded place we could settle into but there was no privacy to speak of anywhere. We ended up parking near one of the lakes and spent more than an hour fooling around in the car like a couple of high school teenagers. It was only our second date but I was completely comfortable with him. He never felt like a stranger. From the moment we first touched, I sensed that he was no stranger. My soul immediately recognized his. I had wondered if there would be a spark but that day I discovered that this was far beyond a simple spark. With every kiss and every touch, it became more and more apparent to me that there was an elaborate display of fireworks going off between us. It was as if an ancient but dormant connection suddenly ignited into a fiery explosion of passion. I still replay some of those moments in my mind from time to time and continue to be awed by how effortlessly we clicked that day and every day since then.

Even though we had talked a lot about our sexual desires and what we wanted to explore with each other, I suggested the public park for our second date in order to test our comfort levels and determine if there was enough of a spark to warrant a more intimate hotel date in the future. I never expected that I would want to hasten that process up very much but our teenage-like date in the park changed everything. Once that passion was uncorked, it could not be tamed. Craving him so intensely came as quite a shock to me. The one-week wait between our park date and the next suddenly felt like an eternity.

In the days that followed, our communication began to increase at an alarming rate. We went from chatting briefly one or two times a day about topics covering only either highly sexual or superficial content to chatting several times a day with our conversation topics expanding into far more intimate domains. We were getting to know each other on a deeper level and sharing some of our darkest secrets, fears, and desires with one another. I felt torn between the intoxicating thrill of studying the heart and mind of the most fascinating man I had ever met and a persistent sense of dread that accompanied the idea of becoming emotionally invested in him.

Despite having never felt an emotional connection to any man in my past, I inherently knew that this time would be different. I recognized that this particular slope was far more slippery than I could have ever anticipated and that I was potentially at serious risk to fall in love with a married man, which obviously would not be an ideal situation and could lead to some massive heartache down the road. The emotional red flags were waving at full force by that point but fate had already put the wheels in motion and fear alone was no match for the momentum or the curiosity and passion that propelled it.

Wayne and I both took a day off from work the following week so that we could meet again for longer and in a more private setting. We met at a Winn Dixie parking lot where I left my car and got into his. Wayne drove across the street to a motel and I waited in the car while he got us a room. I was shocked to be so calm. I expected to be nervous in anticipation of physical exploration with a new partner but instead I was eager to get him behind closed doors.

The passion was so intoxicating that it occupied my every resource, leaving no energy left for anything but to enjoy the moment with him as fully as possible. We walked into the room, shed everything but our smiles, and slipped into bed next to each other. The theory was that we would spend the day having crazy, casual sex but reality decided to take a different route. After some fiery foreplay, it became apparent that Wayne's body was experiencing a certain amount of stage fright.

Wayne was humiliated and frustrated but in retrospect I think that was fate's way of pushing us in the right direction. Had Wayne been able to "perform" normally that day, we might have had one exciting escapade and never see each other again. Instead, we spent the day touching, kissing, caressing, and gazing into each other's eyes while sharing stories about our children, our marriages, and the lessons we had learned from it all. Wayne was convinced that I would never want to see him again because he thought I had been dissatisfied with him sexually but he was as wrong as I was in thinking that sexual satisfaction was the objective in the first place.

Our first hotel date that day led to a crucial revelation for me: apparently it wasn't just sexual satisfaction that I was after, at least not with Wayne. I left that hotel room feeling satisfied in every way imaginable. Wayne's touch penetrated much more than my body. Spending that day with him was magical on so many levels.

Wayne awakened something more than passion within me. Describing it in words has always been a challenge even for a word lover like me. The best way I can explain it is by saying that when my spirit collided with Wayne's that day, it felt like something shifted into place on a cosmic level. It was as if I had been sleepwalking through my entire life until he walked into it and snapped me out of that slumber. Suddenly I was alive like never before. Wayne's presence somehow shut down my autopilot mode and allowed me to be fully present in the moment as it happened. In the past, I had only been able to experience this in painfully short, fleeting episodes that seemed to vanish before I could fully appreciate them but with Wayne, it was as though time slowed to a crawl and I had the opportunity, the energy, and the focus to savor every sliver of each moment while we were in them. Still drunk with passion and a strange, but oh so sweet delirium, Wayne drove me back to the parking lot where we parted ways and reluctantly returned to our respective prisons.

Unbeknownst to us, fate sprinkled the seeds of a rare and true love into our hearts that day in the hopes that we might decide to water them and let it flourish. Luckily for us, we did not take that opportunity for granted. From our first meeting in the coffee shop and for another six months afterwards with minimal exceptions for extenuating circumstances, Wayne and I saw each other at least once a week. We would meet at our Winn Dixie parking lot every Wednesday after work and spend at least a couple of hours wrapped up in each other's arms, safely cocooned behind a hotel room door. Every now and then we would take another day off from work and extend our time together.

Time was such a contradiction for me then. When we were together, it seemed to stand still but at the same time, it was never enough and always slipped through our fingertips far too quickly. The days between each of our rendezvous consisted of endless KIK conversations that ranged from mundane chatter of daily life to deep musings about the meaning of life and love and everything in between. Despite an initial attempt at denial and resistance, I fell hopelessly in love with Wayne during those months and agonized endlessly over what I thought was the impossibility of us ever being together outside of the top-secret love nest we had built.

I was a sea of contradictions during those whirlwind months. My heart bounced like a ping-pong ball from love to hope to fear then doubt and back to love again; being healed and then broken all over again by the same force on what felt like an infinite loop of light and dark. I loved him fiercely, but was that enough to navigate the excess baggage we each carried? Was there a chance that Wayne and I could ever be legitimately together? Could our love withstand the drama of dissolving two marriages with children involved or the social upheaval that could come from my family and friends learning that the woman they had always known as a lesbian was now head over heels in love with a man?

Wayne and I had not even openly admitted our feelings to each other. Neither of us wanted to put any unnecessary pressure on the other so we tiptoed carefully around conversations about feelings when it came to each other. But there was no need for words between us. I knew and I knew that he knew too. I could see it in his eyes and feel it in his touch. I tried not to hold his gaze too long for fear that my eyes might betray me and reveal what my lips were too afraid to speak at the time. Our hearts collided and we both inherently knew that no matter what the future held for us, neither of us would ever be the same again.

# CHAPTER 3: EMOTIONAL ROLLER COASTER

The six-month duration of my affair with Wayne was the most incredible and also the most tumultuous time of my life. On the one hand, it was a wild, magical adventure with a man who set my soul on fire and colored my world more beautifully than ever before. On the other hand, though, it was a dark, confusing, frustrating, and terrifying time. Nobody in my life knew about Wayne. Not even my mom, whom I typically shared everything with, or any of my closest friends. Not being able to talk to anyone about Wayne or anything that was happening with him made it even more difficult because I had to keep it all bottled up inside and wasn't able to gather input from people whose opinions I valued. But I recognized how dangerous it would be to share my truth with anybody, including the people I trusted most. It was too big of a secret, too potentially life altering to risk it leaking before I was ready to deal with the inevitable repercussions of it.

Making sense of what I was feeling during those first few months was a major struggle for me. Wayne was the only person I could talk to about it but that, too, was severely limited by the sensitivity of the circumstances we were in. I weighed my words carefully with Wayne for longer than I wanted to. Even though I always felt like I could freely tell him anything, I was also acutely conscious of how what I chose to share with him might affect him or his family. It seemed clear that he did not love his wife or want to be with her but he was concerned about how leaving her would impact his son or his parents and I did not want to influence that decision for him one way or the other. If he decided to leave Lorena, I wanted it to be because it was the right decision for him and not because he thought I expected or wanted him to.

A month into our affair, I was scheduled to go on vacation with my family and some friends. It was bad enough that said vacation was going to prevent me from seeing Wayne that week but the fact that I would not be able to communicate with him either weighed heavily on me. I didn't want to tell Wayne how much I expected to miss him for fear that it might make things awkward but the idea of being out of communication with him for so many days was a major stressor for me in the days leading up to the trip. The day of my departure, I couldn't help myself and sent him an email: a short but sweet admission that he would be missed.

That time away from Wayne confirmed that no matter how hard I willed him to be nothing more than a plaything to distract me from my miserable marriage, Wayne was slowly but surely chipping away at the walls I had built around my heart. I spent nearly every waking moment of that trip thinking about Wayne and replaying moments we had shared. When I wasn't happily reliving the sensation of his lips on mine or the feeling of his arms around me, I was wracking my brain to try and figure out what was going on with me.

I knew that I was falling for Wayne but admitting that to myself without feeling a sense of panic over it was certainly not a quick or painless process.

As I began to accept that my feelings for Wayne were real and not just infatuation or lust, I started to feel guilty. I had loved Janet once. I see now in retrospect that I no longer loved her by the time I started looking for a new lover but I was in denial at the time and since I did still care for her, I was troubled by the fact that it was getting harder and harder to convince myself that I should stay with her.

I started taking bigger risks by communicating with Wayne, sometimes for hours at a time, while sitting feet away from Janet. The fact that I could literally fall in love with somebody else right under her nose and she never even remotely noticed that anything was off only served to further confirm how beyond repair that marriage was. We were completely disconnected.

Janet may have subconsciously suspected that something was wrong because she suddenly started attempting to initiate more intimacy between us, which was out of character for her throughout most of our relationship. Our lack of intimacy was one of the main things that had motivated me to look for those needs to be met elsewhere. Had she made those changes before I met Wayne, I don't know that things would have turned out the way that they did. It took her years to get the message but by the time that she decided to do something about it, I was no longer interested in going there with her.

I started to reject Janet's advances but knew that I would have to give in once in a while in order to avoid suspicion. It led to a major revelation for me when being intimate with Janet made me feel like I was betraying Wayne instead of the other way around. It was overwhelming for me to realize that my loyalties lied more with Wayne than with the woman I was actually married to. I was terrified of the implications because even though I suspected that Wayne felt the same way about me, it seemed unrealistic that he and I could ever be together formally and openly.

I began to brace myself for what I thought was inevitable heartbreak and tried to convince myself that I needed to accept the impossibility of a real relationship with Wayne and start to put some distance between us. During one of our hotel visits, the angel and devil on my shoulder were having a particularly explosive argument over whether or not I should tell Wayne that we needed to stop seeing each other. Nothing of the like ever came out of my mouth but Wayne quickly picked up on my confused energy. He kept asking me what was wrong. I wasn't ready to answer him so I kept dismissing it as nothing but he and I both knew that something was shifting. The only thing I could manage to tell him was that I was worried about explosions. He assumed that I meant the possible explosions that would result if his wife or mine discovered our relationship but that was only a small part of it for me. The explosion I feared most was the way I imagined my heart would burst when faced with the reality that Wayne and I could never be together outside of our beloved cocoon. I couldn't bring myself to tell him that, though, so instead I just rambled on and on about explosions and us being crazy for doing what we were doing.

That day, I also started dropping hints to Wayne that work was going to begin getting hectic and might prevent me from seeing him as often in the coming months. My mind was still trying to convince my heart that I had to let Wayne go. The practical part of me believed that our situation was unsustainable and that I might as well end it gracefully before things got dramatic but my heart refused to accept that kind of logic. When I listened carefully enough, my heart insisted that I had it all wrong and that it was actually my wife, not Wayne, who I needed to walk away from.

Wayne and I began hypothesizing about the possibility of going away together. As much as I longed for an opportunity to fall asleep and wake up next to Wayne or to walk around in public holding his hand without looking over my shoulder or stressing about who might be watching us, it seemed almost as impossible as us being together like a normal couple. Wayne had a lot of physical distance from Lorena that made it easier for him to get away but my situation was considerably different. Janet was highly dependent on me and kept me on a pretty tight leash so I wasn't sure I would be able to pull off a trip that she wouldn't insist on being a part of. I enjoyed entertaining the idea but didn't really take it seriously at first. Wayne kept bringing it up and suggesting different places we could go but I usually responded by blowing it off as nothing more than a nice idea that would be unlikely to manifest in reality. I really wanted to go away with him but there were a lot of thoughts holding me back. What if we went away and things felt awkward? What if he started to annoy me? What if we got caught? Even more frightening was the idea that it might confirm how right we were for each other and then it would be too hard to go back to our cocoon. I think in the back of my mind, I understood that going away with him would permanently alter our circumstances so I avoided it for several months. But as Wayne was losing hope that I would ever go away with him, I was spending more and more time trying to figure out how I could potentially make it happen.

One day while in the middle of a fight with Janet over something trivial, I spontaneously decided to use the fight as a catalyst for the elusive trip. I told Janet that I would be taking some time for myself in the coming weeks, that I desperately needed space and time away from her so that I could figure things out. She was stunned. I wasn't asking her permission or leaving any room for ifs, and, or buts. I made it clear that my unhappiness was at an all-time high and I was going to take a weekend away from her whether she liked it or not. Janet reluctantly accepted my announcement and that effectively ended our argument. I don't think she took me seriously at first. She probably assumed that I had just reacted out of anger and would soon change my mind about going anywhere without her so she didn't mention it again and seemed to be making an effort to be on her best behavior, as if that would help me to forget how miserable we were together.

Over the next couple of weeks, I tried to figure out where Wayne and I could go and what I would tell Janet. Wayne was happy that I had finally agreed to go away with him, though he was still skeptical about whether or not I was actually going to go through with it. We reasoned that it would be best to fly to another city in order to minimize the possibility of bumping into somebody we knew. Eventually we decided that we were going to travel to Arizona. He would tell his wife that he was going to a conference for work and I would tell mine that I was going to visit an old friend from high school who she had met but did not know very well. Our escape from the cocoon plan was officially hatched and in motion.

Once Janet realized that I really was going to go somewhere without her, I noticed a visible shift in her behavior. She seemed concerned that my leaving would end our relationship and tried to convince me to stick around and try to resolve things together rather than by me going away to do all the thinking on my own but I was not about to let her derail the master plan. No matter how much she begged and pleaded (and she did plenty of that), I was determined to make that weekend happen at all costs.

# CHAPTER 4: FREEDOM FLIGHT

Six months after we first began our affair, Wayne and I spun a tangled web of lies with our respective families so that we could spend a full, uninterrupted weekend together. Stepping out of our cocoon and going on a trip with each other was a pivotal moment for both Wayne and me. It was a huge risk for me personally but one that I ultimately decided would be worthwhile regardless of the outcome.

Part of what held me back from taking that leap with Wayne sooner was that I wanted to be sure that I was ready to let go of my wife for the right reasons. I did not want to leave her for him; I wanted to leave her for me. I had to do a lot of soul searching in order to get there and it was tough to navigate through that. I had to juggle the intense sadness, anger, and bitterness of my failed marriage with the joy, passion, and hope of my new relationship with Wayne. Separating those two extremes was obviously challenging but it was important for me to end my marriage because its grass was already officially dead and not just because I thought the grass might be greener with Wayne.

It took me some time, a whole lot of sleepless nights, and a pretty good collection of tears before I finally reached the point where I understood, with certainty and independent of my feelings for Wayne (however powerful they were), that leaving Janet was the best option both for me and for my daughter. I spent years worrying about the effect that a broken family might have on Lea and her emotional welfare but in that moment of clarity, I realized that the truly broken family is the one that tries to force pieces of ill-suited puzzles into places they don't belong. No, my daughter would no longer watch her two miserable mothers try to beat a dead horse. Instead, Lea would learn the importance of refusing to settle for less than she deserves and of doing the right thing even when it happens to also be the scariest. Once I accepted the fate of my marriage for what it was, I was then ready to step outside of the cocoon with Wayne. I was eager, more than anything else, for the chance to get a taste of what it was like to fall asleep and wake up with him by my side. I've affectionately dubbed that weekend getaway our "freedom flight" because that it precisely what it turned out to be.

We booked our flight at the same time but not together. Wayne offered to get my ticket but I was worried about our names being linked on any official document so I suggested that instead we both buy them online at the same time and coordinate so that we purchase seats right next to each other.

There were a couple of weeks between the day we bought our plane tickets and the day we would finally set off on our long awaited cocoon escape. The day before I was scheduled to leave, Janet turned up the heat. She called me in tears and begged me not to go. We spent hours arguing over that trip with her alternating between using anger and guilt to try and convince me to stay. Eventually when she realized that

I wasn't going to change my mind, she gave up and switched gears to play the role of the supportive wife. Suddenly she went from being broken up or angry about it to understanding why I needed space and agreeing to give it to me without further argument. I suspect that she saw the end was near at that point and was trying to avoid pushing me over the edge.

When the big day finally arrived, I could hardly contain myself. The plan was for Wayne and I to both work half a day and then meet at the airport later that afternoon. Focusing on work was nearly impossible. I had butterflies and pretty much the whole zoo in my stomach in anticipation of our trip. I was stressed about leaving everything just right at the house because Janet was not very independent and I wanted to be sure that she could handle the weekend caring for Lea and our pets without incident. I was also stressed about keeping my story straight and not getting caught. The truth is so much easier than having to keep track of all the details in a lie but obviously the circumstances did not allow for transparency.

Having to lie to people that I cared about sucked but it was the only way I could maintain the peace while I tried to sort things out and figure out which direction to take. The butterflies were also fluttering over the idea that Wayne and I were about to get more intimate than ever by sharing space for much longer than we were used to. My gut predicted that there would be no issues and that we would continue to connect as effortlessly as we always had inside of our cocoon but of course there was always the possibility that things could go sour too. Only time would tell which way the pendulum might swing.

In those hours between leaving work and getting to the airport, my stress was bouncing off the charts. I sent Wayne a message when I left my job and then went home to get everything ready. I had a mental checklist to go through in preparation for being absent the entire weekend and also to ensure that my story would not develop any unforeseen holes. I went to Janet's job to let her know that I was heading to the airport and to say goodbye. She took it relatively well and asked me to keep in touch as much as possible. After I got through airport security, I messaged Wayne to let him know where I was and waited for him to arrive. Unbeknownst to me until much later, Wayne was worried that I was going to bail on him. He never let on at the time but apparently because I hadn't messaged him between leaving my job and arriving at the airport, he was under the impression that I was going to get cold feet and leave him hanging at the airport. Once the decision had been made to go on that trip, though, I never even remotely considered backing out. I was ready to see what might come of a weekend alone with the only man who had ever managed to occupy a space in my heart. I knew that the trip was likely to change everything, which is what made it as terrifying as it was exciting.

Walking together through the airport and towards our gate was awkward. We weren't used to being seen so publicly and though we wanted to hold hands, we were still too close to home to take that chance. It felt like we were walking with a spotlight shining on us. Once we got on the plane, though, we both visibly relaxed a bit and got a little closer. We held hands and cuddled close for the duration of the flight.

When we got to Arizona, we picked up the rental car, which happened to be a Jeep and this was ironic to us because we had just been talking about Jeeps and how much I liked them sometime earlier so we had a good laugh over that little piece of synchronicity. Our arrival at the hotel yielded another memorable moment. The woman who checked us in at the hotel took us by surprise when it was Wayne checking in but she asked me for my name too. I automatically replied with my first name so when she asked me for my last name, I panicked, worrying that this would then put us both on record as being together there so I hesitated briefly before using Wayne's last name instead of my own. I'm sure she noticed that Wayne and I were both flustered by her question but luckily she didn't ask me for identification.

As we headed towards our room, I repeated my name with Wayne's last name again in my head a few times and noticed that I really liked the sound of it. I felt a slight twinge of sadness as I lamented the fact that we would never share a family name but then quickly pushed the idea out of my mind so that I could enjoy the weekend with him. Our time was already limited so I didn't want to waste it being sad about things that were beyond my control. Those precious few days were nothing short of magical. We took a walk that night to a Spanish restaurant nearby where we enjoyed a delicious, romantic dinner at an outdoor table with a beautiful view. It was the first time that we were free to act like a normal couple without having to be paranoid about it and the experience easily surpassed my expectations.

Our interaction outside of the cocoon was unsurprisingly as natural as it was in it. Falling asleep in Wayne's arms that night and then waking up with him still by my side was a dream that I never wanted to wake up from. We spent the next two days alternating between exploring the area and each other. Neither of us wanted it to end but Sunday snuck up on us anyway.

The drive back to the airport was filled with the same sense of dread I used to feel when we would head back to the Winn Dixie parking lot from our secret hotel dates. A dark cloud loomed over us both as we waited for our flight. Even the pre-flight drinks were unable to lift our spirits. We found ourselves being slowly pushed from the euphoria of our romantic getaway into an abyss of sadness as time inched us closer towards the inevitable return to the homes and lives we shared with our wives. My heart broke a little when we stepped foot onto the return flight home and a little more shortly afterwards when I saw tears falling from Wayne's eyes as we prepared for landing. Having shared so many happy and passionate hours with Wayne made the idea of having to return to my tense and broken marriage extra brutal. The path from the airport gate where Wayne and I exchanged our goodbyes to the car where Janet was waiting for me was paved with dread.

# CHAPTER 5: THE UNRAVELING

I hadn't missed Janet at all during my trip with Wayne. Even if I hadn't been with Wayne, being away from Janet for a few days was such a tremendous relief that heading back to her at that moment felt a lot like walking the plank. I got into the car beside her and she was clearly happy to see me but I did not feel even remotely the same. Without meaning to, I cringed when she showered me with hugs and kisses and told me how much she had missed me. I'm not sure if she noticed because she never said anything but it became painfully clear to me in that moment that there was no turning back for me anymore. It was a lot to process and I was much quieter than usual on the drive home as I tried to sort through all of my conflicting emotions. I told Janet that I was tired and just wanted to go to bed once we got back to the house.

As I lay next to Janet that night, longing for the feeling of Wayne's arms around me and uncomfortable with Janet's proximity to me, I came to the conclusion that I could no longer maintain the charade. No matter how hard it would be to get the words out or how guilty I might feel about her reaction, the time had come to officially end my marriage. I knew then that there was no possibility for reconciliation with Janet. Though there were years when I longed for a solution and begged her to go to therapy with me or do something to try and resolve our issues, by that point I was done and was no longer interested in even attempting to fix what was clearly beyond repair. It's true that Wayne and my relationship with him served as a catalyst for my initiating the divorce process when I did because if it weren't for him, I likely would have languished in the unhappy marriage for several more years, but I'm certain the outcome would have been the same regardless.

The following day was a Monday and I spent the entire day trying to plan how I would start the conversation with Janet. First, I alerted my parents and best friend of my plans. I think they were all relieved but my parents suggested that I wait until after the holidays in order to avoid tension and awkwardness at Christmastime, which was right around the corner, but I knew that waiting was not an option. I had already prolonged the inevitable long enough and at that point felt literally unable to fake it even one minute longer.

I decided that the deed would be done the following day after work. I made arrangements for my parents to stay with Lea so that I could speak privately with Janet after we both got out of work. After everything was set, I messaged Wayne and told him of my plan. It was important to me that he know what was going on but I also wanted to make it clear that I had no expectations for him to do the same with his wife. Obviously I wanted him to leave Lorena but I wanted that to be his decision based on what he truly wanted and not because he felt pressured by the action I was planning to take in my own marriage. I was skeptical that Wayne would leave his wife at all so I had internally accepted that he and I would simply continue our weekly covert meetings until one or both of us tired of the arrangement. He asked me repeatedly if I was sure about leaving Janet, which I was. Wayne says now that he was jumping for joy inside when I told him that I was leaving her but he definitely tried to downplay that to me at the time. We were both trying to avoid pressuring each other unnecessarily. We already had enough on our plates and didn't want to add to each other's stress.

Tuesday was D-day and when it arrived, I felt a strange mixture of anxiety and anticipation. I was not looking forward to the deed itself, but I was definitely looking forward to the relief that would likely follow. I spent the day rehearsing a speech in my head about how I would break the news, but when the time came, Janet sensed what was happening before I could even say anything. When she got home from work and realized that our daughter wasn't there because I wanted to talk privately, Janet knew what was coming. She asked if I was leaving her and broke out into a series of screams and sobs when I confirmed that I was. It broke my heart to see Janet suffering like that. It was that kind of reaction that had kept me from following through all of the other times that I had tried to leave her before then. I would feel guilty for making her cry and eventually she would convince me that things weren't that bad and would get better. I would stay and things would usually get better for a few days or maybe even weeks (depending on how determined she thought I was to really leave) but no matter how long the alleged change would last, it would always revert back to business as usual and the whole vicious cycle of unhappiness would start all over again.

Janet most likely thought that this would be just another reset and that she could convince me to keep "trying" but what she did not know was that this time was different. She was distraught. She begged me not to give up on us or on our family, trying to convince me once again that things would get better. When she saw that I wasn't backing down, she asked if there was someone else. I did not want to lie to her but wanted her to know that our break up was about more than someone else so I didn't answer directly. I told her that our marriage needed to end because we were both consistently unhappy with each other and that neither of us deserves to be miserable for the rest of our lives.

That night was one of the most difficult nights of my life. There was a lot of crying for both of us and not much sleeping for either. Janet moved to the couch that night and I laid in bed alone, weighed down by a world of guilt as I listened to her continue sobbing in the other room. I felt horrible but also a tremendous sense of relief. The ball was officially rolling but I knew that I was still in dangerous territory. Despite my having made it clear that I wanted out of the marriage, I knew that Janet still had hope for things to turn around and that it was up to me to avoid wavering no matter how heavy the guilt might get. The next few weeks would be critical as we began the process of unraveling our lives and establishing a new norm. I expected Janet to resist it, but I was committed to resisting her resistance. It wasn't going to be easy but backing down at that point was not an option. Despite the sadness and the guilt, I fell asleep a little lighter that night, hopeful that the storm ahead would eventually usher in brighter days to come. The freedom flight had inspired me to believe that freedom was actually attainable and even more importantly, that I deserved it.

# CHAPTER 6: DODGING LANDMINES

After I messaged him that I had officially asked Janet for a divorce, Wayne called me to make sure I was okay. It was one of only a handful of times that we had spoken on the phone instead of through text. We spoke for a few minutes and I assured him that I would be okay. I knew that the next few months were going to be a challenge for me personally but I did not want to drag Wayne down with me so I tried to downplay the emotional upheaval I was experiencing.

A couple of days after I left Janet, Wayne told me that he planned to leave Lorena too. I reminded him that I wanted him to make whatever decision was best for him and that I did not want him to feel pressured to leave if he wasn't ready. He claimed to be ready but told me that since his stepdaughter's 18th birthday was coming up, he was going to wait until it passed so that he wouldn't ruin it for her. At the time I was still skeptical that he would actually leave, especially because his plan included putting it off for several weeks. I figured that he would probably just fall back into the routine and be unlikely to go through with it once the time came. That was what I worried about for myself, which is why I knew that I couldn't wait until after the holidays to ask Janet for a divorce. At that point, though, my main focus was on dismantling my marriage as cautiously as possible without risking an unwanted attempt at reconciliation. I wanted Wayne to ask for a divorce and was happy that he said he wanted to but was also ready to accept it if he didn't. My own divorce was taking enough of my energy so I didn't have much left over to worry about Wayne's too.

The weeks between our return from the freedom flight and Christmas were particularly rough on the weekly routine that Wayne and I had established. We didn't get to see each other much as I tried to navigate the increasingly choppy waters at home and he tried to plan his exit strategy. I missed him terribly during those weeks even though we chatted through KIK almost constantly.

I asked Janet to move into the spare bedroom and we did our best to coexist peacefully while preparing for our last and most awkward holiday season together. There was nothing easy or pleasant about it. Tensions grew exponentially as Janet gradually realized that this time was different from the others and that I was serious about moving forward with divorce. There were a few times when she would break down crying and plead with me to reconsider but mostly she would just seethe with anger and we both did our best to avoid each other.

Janet and I decided that despite the separation and impending divorce, we would still host our annual Christmas dinner one last time. We had been hosting Christmas dinner for our families for a few years and did not want to change that too abruptly so we thought it would be best to stick with the original plan for one final dinner together. Though I love spending time with my family, Janet's parents and my parents were not exactly enthusiastic about hanging out with each other. They got along okay for the most part but I would not say that they looked forward to or particularly enjoyed spending time together. In retrospect I can see that they really only tolerated each other for her sake and mine.

The tension was obviously at an all-time high during that last Christmas dinner. Everybody was visibly uncomfortable. Conversations were awkward and forced. Nobody was talking about the elephant in the room but we all felt the pressure of his weight on our chests. Everyone ate quickly and unsurprisingly decided to leave shortly afterwards. The whole thing lasted about two hours tops.

The moment our families left, Janet started trying to pick a fight with me. After Lea went to sleep, Janet blew up at me in a blind rage. She was frustrated that I was giving up on us; I was frustrated that she seriously thought there was still an "us" to give up on.

It was hard to sleep that night and even harder to swallow the bittersweet pill of our last Christmas morning as a family. I was undoubtedly ready to leave my marriage but contrary to what Janet believed, that did not make the process any easier on me. I felt guilty for hurting her and knowing that the months ahead were going to be harder on her than on me. Not because she was so in love and heartbroken, but because it would force her to leave her comfort zone and become more independent, which was something she had desperately tried to avoid until then. Janet wasn't happy with me; she was comfortable and wanted to keep it that way even though she probably knew deep down just like I did that we could probably never be happy together again. My relief was greater than my guilt, though, so there was no way that I was going to let her or anyone else convince me that I could do anything other than keep moving forward with the divorce at that point.

The week after Christmas, I asked Janet to move out of the house and gave her a few suggestions on how to make that happen. I also started trying to talk to her about severing our joint accounts and I let her know that I was planning to go see a lawyer for the divorce process. I know it was a lot for her to take in but she handled it pretty well considering. Looking back, I think she was hoping that if she just gave me some time and space, I might miss her and reconsider the divorce. Whatever her reasons, I'm glad that she agreed to move out without making a huge deal about it. Janet didn't waste any time and soon made arrangements to move in with a friend of hers within two weeks.

In the meantime, I had only gotten to see Wayne once or twice for a quick lunch. We still spent the better part of each day chatting with each other but I was under a lot of stress and my focus was on getting Janet out of the house and making an appointment with my lawyer to get some advice on how to proceed. Wayne was still making plans to leave Lorena sometime near the end of January. He seemed like a broken record for a while, asking me repeatedly if I wanted to be single or date freely now that I was headed for divorce. I assured Wayne that the only thing I wanted was to be with him if it was a possibility but that I would understand and accept it if he decided to stay with Lorena.

It's true that I wanted to be with him but I was still not convinced that it would ever actually happen. I thought that there was too much drama in the way for a relationship between us to ever work long term. A new relationship born into the wake of not one but two divorces seemed about as promising as a delicate flower trying to bloom while surrounded by nothing but cement. Despite doubting our viability as a real couple, though, I was completely at peace with the uncertainty that threatened the possibility of any kind of future between Wayne and me. That was strange for me. I had worried about the future with everyone I had ever loved or even strongly liked before Wayne. I had even obsessed over it to a fault in some cases. But with Wayne it was different. Though I loved him more intensely than I had ever loved anyone before, I discovered that this love was unique in other ways too. It was enough to simply love him. I wanted Wayne to be mine officially but I knew that I would continue to love him even if he remained out of reach and that was somehow okay. It was never about owning him. It has only ever been about loving him without condition or expectation. I wanted only what was best for him and what made him happy. If that happened to be me then I welcomed it with open arms and a heart full of gratitude but I would have accepted any outcome with nothing but love and understanding for the incredible man that he is. Not to mention a deep appreciation for the impact he had made on my life and in my heart. I knew that no matter what happened between Wayne and me at that point, my life was better because of him and I would always be grateful to him for that.

As New Year's Eve approached, Wayne and I lamented the fact that we could not be together to usher in the New Year and all of the dramatic changes that loomed on its horizon for us both. He had plans to celebrate at home with Lorena and his family and I had plans to watch the ball drop on TV with Janet and Lea. I recall that New Year's Eve clearly. I sat on the couch across from Janet while Lea played at the coffee table. The television was on but Janet and I were both on our phones as usual. I'm not sure what she was up to on hers but I was going back and forth between reading poetry online and messaging Wayne. It was awkward for me to be there with Janet but I knew Wayne was having a harder time. He was trying to keep it cool via text but I could sense his emotional turbulence just the same. He was drinking and I worried that the alcohol was making him more careless since he was messaging me a lot when he should have been interacting with Lorena and his family to avoid suspicion.

Once Lea fell asleep, Janet and I talked a bit about the changes that were to come. I assured her that I was committed to making the transition as painless as possible for her and for our daughter. She made it clear that she had hopes for us to reconcile in the future. I didn't want to hurt her more than I already had but I also didn't want to give her any false hope so

I told her that while I could not predict the future, I was certain that we needed to go our separate ways. I went to bed that night missing Wayne but hopeful about the New Year and the opportunity to rewrite my life story.

Wayne shocked me the next morning when he messaged me to let me know that he had asked Lorena for a divorce the night before. Despite his plan to wait at least a few more weeks, drinking his way into the New Year while in her presence convinced him that it couldn't wait. My heart danced happily at the news but also worried about Wayne. Something told me that Lorena was not the understanding type and that she was not going to make things easy on him. I knew that things were likely to get dramatic but I also knew there wasn't anything I wasn't willing to endure if it meant that I could be with Wayne. For the first time since Wayne and I met, I felt a glimmer of hope about the possibility that we might someday be a regular couple.

# CHAPTER 7: COMING OUT OF NEW CLOSETS

I came out of the closet as a lesbian when I was a teenager. Twenty years later, I found myself trapped in a new kind of closet. Obviously the lesbian label no longer fit me. Falling in love with Wayne essentially kicked me out of the lesbian club, so to speak, but nobody knew it other than Wayne and me. Being in the closet is not a good feeling, no matter what the skeletons in that closet happen to made of. I had been with only women for so long that I knew coming out as being in a heterosexual relationship at this stage in my life would confuse many and possibly anger some. I also knew that many people in my life would assume my relationship with Wayne was doomed and that I would eventually get bored of him and return to dating women.

I had struggled so much to come out of the closet the first time around that I wasn't thrilled about the notion of being back in another one. I started growing eager to share my big news with people I love but also recognized that it was important to time it properly too. More specifically, I wanted to focus on getting Janet out of the house before making a move to step out of my closet because if she were to get wind of it before moving, it would make the living situation unbearable for all of us.

Two weeks into the New Year, I helped Janet to

move out of the house and into the home she was going to share with a friend. In the process, Janet's new roommate sat me down and tried to convince me that it was only temporary. According to her, now that Janet was out of the house, we could use the space and time to heal our relationship and start from scratch by dating again. I made it clear to her that I had no intention of dating Janet or in reconciling our relationship.

A few days after moving, Janet asked me to go to therapy with her. Of course she never considered it all those years when I begged her to go to therapy with me in an effort to save our relationship but once I finally left, she was suddenly ready and willing to give it a try. I told Janet that we were already beyond the point where therapy could be of any help for our marriage but suggested that we both attend individually. Since I knew she would never do it on her own, I contacted a therapist, set up an appointment for her, and drove her to her first session. I was glad that Janet agreed to go for herself even if she was only doing it for me at first. I was worried about her and wanted to make sure that she had some kind of support in place. Janet wasn't the only one who needed help, though, and I wasn't too proud to admit that. It was a struggle for me to process all of my emotions and I still had a lot of uncertainty ahead as I prepared to come out of the closet in reverse. I knew it was almost time to tell some of my closest friends and family members about Wayne but I wasn't sure how they would take the news. There was no doubt that the people who mattered would come to accept him if they saw how happy he made me but I also knew that there would be a great deal of shock to contend with initially, especially from my parents.

I scheduled my own appointment with a different therapist so that I could get some professional guidance as I prepared to literally turn my whole life upside down. All of my relationship experience in the past had been with women so obviously it was going to make some serious waves as I began to publicize both the impending divorce from Janet and my newfound love for a member of the opposite sex who also happened to be getting ready to go through a divorce of his own. The timeline would naturally be confusing to most, particularly since our relationship was presumed to be much newer than it actually was.

Wayne and I started to slowly but surely unravel our cocoon. We reinstated our weekly routine of hotel dates followed by lunch but we no longer had the shroud of secrecy hanging over our heads so we switched from our hidden lunch spot to more public places and were more open with our affection. It was a strange but very welcome feeling to not be looking over my shoulder every time he held my hand or pulled me close. Neither of us was divorced yet but we had finally taken steps toward that freedom and had done so together. We both understood that the divorces would be challenging and some type of drama was likely to erupt along the way but we were hopeful that our love was strong enough to see us through it.

One afternoon, Lea and I met up with Wayne for

lunch. It was the first time she met Wayne but Lea accepted him instantly and he was great with her. I knew without a doubt that no matter how difficult things might get, there was nothing I wanted more than to be in a relationship with Wayne.

There was a party coming up at the end of the month and I invited Wayne to join me for it as my date. It was a big deal because many of my friends were going to find out about Wayne for the first time and some of them didn't even know that me and Janet had split up yet so those were in for an even bigger surprise. I was nervous about how that would play out but I was ready to move Wayne from his position as my biggest secret to a much more prominent role as the greatest love my life has ever known. The party served as a deadline of sorts for me. I had two weeks to break the news to my parents and my best friend before letting the cat out of the bag by attending the party with him.

I scheduled a breakfast date with my best friend, Hilary, a few days later. Despite having rehearsed what I was going to say a million times, it was hard to get anything out once I was sitting in front of her. Hilary knew that I had something to tell her but had no idea what it was about. When I was hesitant, she started jumping to conclusions and assumed that I was going to tell her that I planned to get back together with Janet, which she would have been adamantly against. I assured her that getting back together with Janet was not an option so she relaxed. I then told her that the reason I would never get back together with Janet is because I had fallen hopelessly in love with somebody else and that immediately peaked her interest.

Hilary wanted to know everything about "her," which of course reminded me of how shocking the news would be to anybody who knew me. Since I couldn't spit it out, I told Hilary that I was just going to show her a picture and handed her my phone with a picture that I had taken of Wayne and me while we were on our secret getaway. I wish I had taken a picture of Hilary's face when she looked at the photo. Initially she thought it was a prank and joked about where I had hidden the cameras. A few minutes later when she realized that I was serious, Hilary picked her jaw up from the floor and proceeded to ask me a million questions about him, how we met, and how I had come to fall in love with him. I told her the entire story from beginning to end and did not bother to hold back any details. It was cathartic to finally share my truth with someone and I felt confident that my secret was safe with her. While she was shocked about me having fallen in love with a man, Hilary was happy for me and excited to meet the mysterious man who had stolen my heart. I knew that I could count on her to support me and felt confident that my other genuine friends would be just as supportive. Hilary and I agreed to have a double date before the party so that she could be the first of my friends to officially meet Wayne.

Though I had opened up to Hilary without reservations, Wayne and I had a different plan for how to bring our relationship out of the closet to everyone else. Somehow, admitting that we had been having an affair with each other for several months before leaving our wives was not something we were eager to share with the world at large. We came up with a less scandalous story in which we allegedly met on the plane during our weekend getaway. The problem with this romanticized story about the serendipity of two strangers sitting next to each other on a plane is that there was an obvious discrepancy between the timeline of that story and our level of comfort and familiarity with each other. We did not seem like two people who had recently met and for those who knew us well, it likely wouldn't be too hard to figure out that we were already very much in love with each other. We decided to stick with that story anyway, though, and try to point the focus more towards how happy we are together rather than how the relationship began.

I am not ashamed of how Wayne and I met. In fact, I think it's pretty amazing that such a powerful love was born from such ethically questionable beginnings. It goes to show how a love that is meant to be can overcome even the most challenging of circumstances. We thought it was best, though, to sugarcoat the story a bit so as to avoid increasing the existing levels of drama with our wives as we fumbled through not one but two divorces.

Hilary loved Wayne when she and her girlfriend, Mary, met up with us for dinner. They both admitted that it was a little weird to see me being affectionate with a man but that they were happy to see me so happy for a change. After Hilary met Wayne, I started thinking about how to tell my parents about him, which was the revelation I was most apprehensive about. My parents were completely supportive of my lesbian relationships and my mom was a strong advocate of the LGBT community but neither of them understood bisexuality. Each of them had commented to me on separate occasions about how they could understand that some people are gay or lesbian but that what really confused them were people who claimed to be bisexual. According to my parents, sexuality was black or white and they thought the gray area in between was simply a purgatory for gays and lesbians who had not yet come to fully accept their own homosexuality. I never thought this way myself. I have always believed that sexuality is fluid and that there is a lot more gray area than there is black or white.

I never identified as bisexual because I could not see myself being emotionally connected to a man even though I was physically attracted to some. I convinced myself that if my attraction to men was only physical, then I must be a lesbian because I wanted a relationship to have more substance than physical attraction alone and I had only been able to develop romantic feelings for women all my life. While I understood and accepted that there was always a possibility that I might feel something for a man, it was so unlikely that I thought I had a better chance of winning the lottery than falling for a man and anybody who knew me came to think along similar lines.

My parents would be shocked to learn that I had somehow met a man who sparked something more than lust in me. I knew that they would be floored by the news and was worried about how they would process the idea of me being in a relationship with a man after so many years of me being with only women.

A few months into my secret relationship with Wayne, my dad found out that an ex of mine was involved with a man and pregnant with his child. This news apparently threw him for a big loop and he kept asking me how she could go from being romantically involved with a woman for so long and then switch to a man just like that. I tried to use that opportunity to explain to him my belief that sexuality is fluid and sometimes doesn't fit into the lines that society prescribes to it. He wasn't having it, though, and made some comment about how if that were true I probably would have fallen in love with a man by then and that was a ridiculous notion to him. It took a lot of tongue biting to avoid spilling the beans to him right then and there but Wayne was still very much a secret at that point and I didn't think my dad could hold on to a secret that big. But that was then and this was now. The time had come for me to let my parents know about Wayne; I just needed to figure out the right way to break the news.

It was no surprise to my mom that I had been dating someone. I needed someone to babysit Lea and Janet was working during my weekly dates with Wayne so I would take Lea to my parents' house and tell them that I was going to dinner or happy hour with friends from work. This worked well enough while I was still with Janet but after the break up, my mom started getting suspicious about my weekly outings.

She asked me directly if I was dating someone and since I didn't want to lie to her more than necessary, I admitted that I was seeing someone special but that I didn't plan on giving her more details than that until I was ready to do so. Much to my surprise, my mom did not give me any grief about my secrecy and instead was thrilled to learn that I was seeing somebody new since she, too, had been worried that I might fall back into old habits with Janet before finalizing the divorce.

There were a few weeks between when I first admitted the existence of a special person to my mom and the day when I was finally ready to tell her more about that person. Those weeks were filled with endless questions from my highly curious mother. She wanted to know if "she" was Hispanic, how old she was, where she was from, and my personal favorite: "is she feminine or butch?" I couldn't help but laugh as I replied, "way more butch than anyone I've ever dated before." I made sure to avoid using any pronouns in my responses to her questions, a strategy which I had perfected before coming out of the closet to announce that I was interested in women back in my teen years. Here I was again, a lifetime later, playing the pronoun game and strategizing how to best come out of the closet, only this time in reverse.

A few days before my first official, public date with Wayne, I went to my parents' house for dinner and planned to tell them about Wayne afterwards. After we ate, I was helping my mom clean up in the kitchen when she gave me a way in by asking me again to tell her more about the girl I was seeing. I asked her to sit down so that we could talk about it. My mom could tell that I was nervous but that confused her since I had never before been hesitant to share anything about my personal life with her. She couldn't figure out why information about my new love interest was such a secret and she asked if I could at least share her name. It was the perfect opportunity to just put it out there so I responded with Wayne's name and braced myself for her reaction. A look of genuine confusion washed over my mom's face as she repeated the name and commented on how odd that name was for a woman. I pointed out that indeed it was an odd name for a woman hoping that she would catch on but instead she said that people were naming their kids in all sorts of weird ways lately.

It floored me that my mom was still so sure that I was talking about a woman. It was absolutely inconceivable to her that I would be dating a man. So much so, as a matter of fact, that when I showed her a picture of Wayne to clarify, she asked if he was transgender. That question really blew my mind because she was entirely serious. The possibility that I could actually be involved with a man was so far removed from her mind that she could not immediately accept it as truth. When I assured her that Wayne was a man from birth and that I was completely serious, my mother was dumbfounded. My truth detonated like a bomb over one of her deepest convictions, shattering her illusions and leaving her in a state of utter confusion.

My mom ran to the other room screaming for my father to come into the kitchen immediately. My dad came quickly, wondering what all the fuss was about, and she asked him to sit down because I had something to tell him about the person I was seeing. She asked me to just show him the picture so I handed it to him and braced for what was sure to be another dramatic reaction. Instead, though, my dad sat there silently with widened eyes shifting between the picture and me. He was literally speechless for several minutes while my mom bombarded me with questions about Wayne, how we met, and how everything came to be.

As much as I wanted to tell my parents the truth, I still didn't feel comfortable sharing the real story with them because I was worried about that truth getting back to Janet and potentially making the divorce far more dramatic than necessary. I told them the story Wayne and I had invented about meeting on the plane and tried to focus more on how I felt about him than the details of our meeting. I left my parents' house that night feeling like the weight of the world was off my shoulders. It was such a relief to finally tell them about Wayne, even if I did have to sugar coat all the gory details of our true meeting and situation.

A few days later, it was time for Wayne and I to officially step out of the cocoon by attending a party together as a couple. Only a few of my closest people knew that he was going to join me but despite their initial surprise and confusion, all of my friends accepted Wayne with relative ease. Some had questions about Janet but many of them expressed that it was nice to see me so happy for a change.

Wayne was great with my friends and made a good impression on everyone he met. Despite not being fond of overly social situations, Wayne is naturally a highly likeable guy because he is genuine and simply awesome all around (I may be a bit biased, but it's still true). The cat was officially out of the bag but I still needed to tread carefully to avoid the news getting back to Janet before I could tell her myself. I felt like it was important for me to be the one she heard it from rather than through the grapevine, but I was worried about how she would take it and the impact it might have on our ability to remain civil through the divorce. I decided to give it a little bit of time before approaching the subject with her.

My parents were growing more and more eager to meet my mystery man so I promised them that I would invite him over for dinner soon. In the weeks that followed, I started seeing a therapist and hired a lawyer to help me get the ball rolling and officially file for divorce. I wanted to get divorced as quickly and painlessly as possible. The sooner it was done, the better off Janet and I would both be. Janet definitely didn't share my enthusiasm about the divorce at the time but now that she is in a better place, I am sure she realizes that it was best for us both after all.

My therapist was extremely helpful in guiding me through the anxiety over all of the intense growing pains that I was experiencing at the time. She gave me great advice on how to process my emotions and it was a major relief to be able to be completely open with her about the whole thing and get the objective opinion of a qualified professional. I was feeling good about my life and looking forward to getting over the divorce and on to brighter days.

Every meeting with my therapist was a cathartic experience and I would share details about each session with Wayne. Much to my surprise, Wayne offered to join me at therapy if I wanted him to. He said that even though things were progressing well between us, we were up against some pretty intense odds and he just wanted me to know that he would be willing to go if I thought it might help. I think I fell in love with him all over again in that moment. I had begged Janet to go to therapy for years to no avail and then this incredible man who I wasn't even having trouble in my relationship with offers to go with me without my even having to ask. It was further affirmation that leaving her and being open to sharing my heart with him was one of the best decisions I have ever made in my entire life.

I took Wayne up on the offer and he joined me for a few sessions with my therapist. She was extremely helpful in giving us advice on how to process our stress and how to best integrate our families and children. My therapist was impressed with how solid our relationship was considering the circumstances under which it began and the rough waters it was being subjected to at the time. She loved that we had developed our own personal relationship constitution and that we were so open and honest with each other about our needs and desires. It was nice for our relationship to be affirmed by someone in a professional capacity and I think it helped give us even more confidence going forward. My therapist gave Wayne and me a few homework assignments, one of which included a test to determine what our individual love languages are. Wayne and I both took the test independently and quickly discovered that we speak the same love language. This, of course, was not much of a surprise to us since Wayne and I have always seemed to be on the same page.

# CHAPTER 8: DRAMA & DECEPTION

Wayne and I were happy but we were also swimming neck deep in drama. Janet was upset that I had filed for divorce and our interactions when exchanging Lea were growing more and more tense each time. Wayne had not officially filed for divorce yet but Lorena was highly emotional and started spending more time at their house than was the norm, presumably in an attempt to get him to change his mind. All her increased presence accomplished, however, was make Wayne more uncomfortable and sparked more frequent conflicts between them.

Wayne was worried about his son, Sebastian, and the impact that the fallout might have on him so he didn't tell him what was going on right away, even though Sebastian was certainly old enough to know better and the tension in the house was not lost on him. Wayne and I had very different ways of approaching our divorces. For me, it was important to move things along as quickly as possible. I felt strongly that the longer it dragged out, the more difficult it would be on Janet, Lea, and me. Wayne, on the other hand, thought that it would be easier on Sebastian, Lorena, and himself if he didn't rush the change. I did not agree with his methodology and warned him that this situation was much like removing a band aid in that the faster you rip it off, the sooner the pain will pass and healing can begin. But he disagreed with me and I had no choice but to respect Wayne's position.

While I was eager for Wayne to move things along both for our sake and for his, I was not about to pressure him to speed things up if he wasn't comfortable doing so. All I could do was offer my advice and support him in whatever he decided. It wasn't easy. I wasn't comfortable with the slow pace Wayne had adopted for his own separation process and had a feeling that it would end up creating far more drama than necessary, but the choice was his to make and I loved him enough to just be there for him even if I didn't agree with the way he was doing things.

At that point, I was completely invested in Wayne so I felt extremely vulnerable because though I knew that he truly loved me, I wasn't entirely convinced that he was going to go through with the divorce. He had stuck it out for his son's sake for so many years that I had to acknowledge the possibility that he might decide to continue doing so. Ultimately I decided that the love I shared with Wayne was worth feeling vulnerable for and taking that risk. I set a time limit of six months in my mind. I decided that for six months, I would support him unconditionally and freely give him my love and commitment. If he did not at least begin the divorce proceedings within that time or make real changes in his living situation, I planned to move him into the friend zone and just be single for a while.

Wayne had no clue about this timeline of mine. I never told him because I didn't want that to influence his decisions in any way. In fact, he still does not know about my timeline and will likely protest when he reads about it in here (sorry, love!). The important thing for me at the time was that I knew Wayne and I loved each other fiercely and I was hopeful that true love would prevail, even if it did have a field of landmines to run through before reaching the happily ever after line.

Eager to escape the drama for a bit, Wayne and I took the day off and spent it lounging near the ocean and enjoying each other's company. I had invited him over to dinner at my parents' house later that night. I was nervous about him meeting them for the first time but also looking forward to it. Unbeknownst to him or me, though, Lorena had caught on to us and been doing a little digging. Apparently the knowledge that there was another woman in the picture was more than she could handle so she began hatching up a desperate scheme to reel him back in.

Lorena called Wayne that day while we were having lunch and asked him if he was at work even though she had driven by and already knew he was not there. Wayne told her that he was not at work and asked her what she wanted. She begged him to come home, insisting it was urgent that they speak in person. When he refused, Lorena dropped a bomb on Wayne by telling him that she had been diagnosed with stage IV cancer. He told her that he was sorry to hear such tragic news. She expected him to drop everything and run to her, but instead he offered his condolences and ended the call.

The conversation between Wayne and Lorena definitely rained on our parade that day. I told Wayne how sorry I was to hear of Lorena's condition and that

I completely understood if he wanted to reschedule our dinner date with my parents, but he insisted that we should continue our day as planned. Since she hadn't displayed any signs of illness before then, Wayne seemed cautiously skeptical about Lorena's announcement of such a dramatic diagnosis. We finished our lunch and then headed to my house to relax a bit before dinner but there was an undeniable heaviness in the air.

The mood shifted as Wayne and I drove into my parents' driveway that night. We walked hand in hand into my parents' house and I introduced Wayne to my mom first and then my dad. I could tell that Wayne was as nervous as I was, but he still managed to make a great first impression. It was such a strange feeling for me to be affectionate with Wayne in front of my parents. I'm sure it was just as strange for them as it was for me. I had boyfriends in high school but never anyone serious enough for me to introduce to my parents as such so this was definitely a first. The fact that I was not only dating Wayne but also that I wanted my parents to meet him spoke volumes about how I felt for him.

My father liked Wayne but was immediately distrustful of his intentions. He couldn't understand what a man would want with a woman who had identified as a lesbian nearly her entire life. I think my dad initially assumed that Wayne was just some guy with a lesbian fetish or some other less than honorable motive for wanting to date me. He was even more apprehensive about Wayne when my mom told him that Wayne was also married and in the process of getting a divorce. It really rubbed my dad the wrong way to think that his daughter was involved with a married man even though his daughter was also technically still a married woman. It bothered my dad so much that he expressly forbade me from brining Wayne to his birthday dinner a couple weeks later.

It really hurt my feelings that my dad would reject Wayne so easily without even knowing any facts about the situation. His reaction made me even less inclined to tell him the truth about how long Wayne and I had really been together because I was worried that he would judge him and me even more harshly than he already had. I didn't tell Wayne how my dad felt at the time because I didn't want to make him feel uncomfortable.

My mom, on the other hand, absolutely loved Wayne and was thrilled to see me so happy. I had warned Wayne that my mom was notorious for having no filter. She says exactly what she's feeling, which is one of those things about her that I have a love-hate relationship with, depending on the situation. A couple of days after meeting him for the first time, my mom showed Wayne what I meant by sending him a friend request on social media followed by a long message about how happy she was to meet him and to see the happiness he was bringing out in me. Had we truly been dating for only a few weeks, I would have been incredibly embarrassed by that and worried that it might scare him off for being too intense too soon, but luckily I was completely comfortable with Wayne then so we just had a good laugh over it. My mom is adorable and simply could not contain her happiness about my happiness.

About a week later, I received a mysterious text from a number that I didn't recognize. The message came early in the morning while I was getting ready for work. The woman, who identified herself as "Kelsey," wanted me to agree to meeting in person or talking on the phone but was initially very cryptic about why she wanted to talk to me. After exchanging a few messages, she claimed to be a friend of Janet's who was allegedly concerned for her and trying to figure out what had happened between us, but when she mentioned that she knew I was already in a new relationship, I knew she couldn't be a friend of Janet's and immediately jumped into defensive mode.

Janet did not yet know about my relationship with Wayne so I doubted that this Kelsey character even knew Janet, let alone had a friendship with her. I refused to meet but we spent the better part of the day exchanging messages as I tried to figure out whom I was really communicating with. Whoever Kelsey was, she seemed to know at least something about Wayne and me and a little about Janet too. She obviously had my phone number. I wasn't sure what else this woman knew about me or why she cared, but I started to suspect that perhaps it was Lorena reaching out to me under a false name. I told Wayne what was going on and sent him some screen shots of the conversation, but he said there was no way it could be Lorena. He didn't recognize the number and seemed certain that she could not have found a way to get in touch with me. I was not so convinced. The mystery woman and I spent nearly the entire day exchanging messages wherein she was desperately trying to convince me that I should get back together with Janet, which only served to confirm for me that she was indeed Lorena.

After a while, it dawned on me that she said something very specific about me having a heart of gold, which I had initially found odd but then realized that this was proof of her true identity. I messaged Wayne and asked him to re-read me the message that my mom had sent him on social media and sure enough, my mom had mentioned me having a heart of gold in her message. It was clear then that Lorena had somehow gotten into Wayne's social media account and read my mom's message to him, which then led her to me. Wayne was shocked that Lorena had reached out to me and tried to convince me to get back together with Janet. I did not find it quite so shocking, though. While I did not know Lorena personally, what I did know about her from Wayne told me that she was a desperate woman who was capable of anything if she thought it might reel him back in.

I felt sorry for Lorena. I wasn't convinced that she had cancer because I thought that it was just a ploy to keep Wayne around but even if she wasn't sick, she was clearly suffering and I felt a sense of guilt for the role I played in that. Once I knew for sure that it was her I was conversing with, I tried my best to make her feel better. I gave her advice about moving on and told her that I was sorry she was struggling so much with it all. I tried my best to be kind and let her know that while I regretted that my relationship with Wayne hurt her, I felt strongly that he and I are meant to be together and was not going to let him go unless he wanted me to do so. Of course she never admitted that she was Lorena even when I called her on it. She stuck with her story the whole time and eventually I simply stopped responding to her messages.

It was an interesting tactic, trying to reunite me with Janet in the hopes that I would break her estranged husband's heart. But when that didn't work, Lorena tried posing as other women and messaging Wayne on KIK. Perhaps she wanted to entice him into illicit messages so that she could then share them with me and cause trouble between us, but Wayne never took the bait. Every time he received a new message from someone, he would tell me and then delete it. Wayne thought it was just random spam from KIK, but I knew it was Lorena trying to figure out a way to come in between us.

Worried that Lorena might beat me to it, I decided that it was time to tell Janet about Wayne. Janet had never been fond of men in any way so I knew that my dating a man would be a harder pill for her to swallow than if I had started dating another woman, particularly because she would be concerned about our daughter. I was anxious about her reaction so at the suggestion of my therapist, I made arrangements to go with Janet to her therapist for a "co-parenting" session in which I was planning to tell her about the new love in my life. Well we spent so much time talking about actual co-parenting issues and concerns that I never found the right way to bring up the topic of Wayne before the session ended. On the way back to my house, though, I told Janet about the text messages I had received from a mysterious woman and then revealed that the woman turned out to be the estranged wife of someone I was seeing. I told her about Wayne and she became enraged. She hurled a few insults my way before offering her opinion on how I had moved on too quickly and that I need to consider the welfare of our daughter, etc. We argued for several minutes before she stormed off and I felt an instant sense of relief. I wasn't happy that Janet was hurting but it was a huge weight off my shoulders that she finally knew Wayne existed and that I didn't have to be paranoid anymore about who might tell her before me. Janet was hurt and she was angry. She said some things that really hurt my feelings, but I understood where she was coming from and was grateful that despite her flaws, she was a decent human being who was not willing to stoop as low as Lorena to get what she wanted.

Lorena, on the other hand, was not a graceful loser by any stretch of the imagination. When she realized that her phony text messages were not working, she decided to shift her focus to the cancer card instead. The more time Wayne spent out of the house, the more Lorena would play up the alleged cancer diagnosis. It became clear to me relatively quickly that Lorena did not have cancer at all. What she had was a relentless desperation to keep him in her life at all costs and in her mind, faking a fatal illness was the only way she could possibly convince him to stay.

There were a few weeks there when I thought

Lorena's evil master plan might be successful. Wayne and his family were suffering at the thought of Sebastian being without a mother and Wayne was clearly struggling with the idea that the divorce might add to her stress while she battled cancer. Wayne admitted to me that he was skeptical about Lorena truly having cancer, but he didn't think she was capable of such a horrible lie. Even if she was capable, he was afraid to call her on it and then risk the possibility of being wrong.

Nevertheless, there were too many things that simply did not add up. Lorena claimed to have stage IV, ovarian cancer, yet her doctors supposedly kept rescheduling appointments, especially when Wayne insisted on going to them with her. Also, she did not look or behave as one would expect from a person who is so near to death's door. Wayne saw those discrepancies too but wanted to tread carefully just in case she was telling the truth. It was really hard for him to accept that Lorena could deliberately do something so callous and cruel to him and his parents, but as the weeks went by and nothing changed, he slowly started coming around to the idea that perhaps he had underestimated her capacity for deception.

Despite my certainty that Lorena was lying about having cancer, I offered my opinion but never pressed Wayne on it because I wanted him to see it for himself. She always had some excuse or another whenever he would question her about the diagnosis. Then one day when she supposedly went to the doctor, Wayne pressured her for the results until she finally sent him something in writing. That was all the confirmation that Wayne needed to know that Lorena had in fact been faking cancer.

The documents that Lorena sent Wayne were undeniably photo shopped. Wayne was both shocked and understandably angry that she would lie so blatantly about something so serious. He told her that he did not believe her, but much like when I called her out via text message, Lorena refused to concede that she had been caught. Luckily Wayne was able to see through the denial and finally come to terms with the reality that it had all been nothing more than a cruel hoax.

The extent of Lorena's cruelty and sheer malice was not revealed until more than a year later when it was discovered that she had even lied to her own son about having cancer in attempt to turn him against his father. Obviously anybody with a conscience or any ethical inclination whatsoever would never fabricate having cancer as a means of emotional manipulation, but sadly Lorena seems to be devoid of both conscience and moral compass. Fortunately, however, Lorena's lack of integrity had gotten her into some legal trouble that gave Wayne a significant advantage in the divorce.

Lorena was on probation and Wayne was aware of several ways in which she was violating said probation, which gave him the upper hand when it came to preventing her from stalling the divorce unnecessarily, though that certainly did not stop her from trying. Wayne filed for divorce shortly after the diagnosis was confirmed to be a hoax, but Lorena took her sweet time producing required documentation or signing off on paperwork as the process moved forward. There were several instances where Wayne had to remind her that he would not hesitate to report her probation violations if she refused to complete her part of the divorce in a reasonable timeframe. Nevertheless she dragged each step as long as she could.

There was a time about halfway into Wayne's divorce process where I started to worry for his safety. Lorena was clearly capable of atrocities that nobody expected from her so the more emotional outbursts she would have towards Wayne or his parents, the more I worried that she might someday snap severely enough to cause him physical harm.

Even after the cancer fiasco, Wayne was still somewhat naïve about what she was capable of. I was shocked when I asked Wayne if he was still sleeping in the same bed with Lorena and Sebastian and he confirmed that he was. When Wayne realized that this stunned me, he assured me that Sebastian slept in the middle and that there was no contact between him and Lorena. Wayne seemed to think that I was jealous, but I made it clear that jealousy had nothing to do with it. I knew that Wayne was not interested in being romantic with Lorena and trusted him completely in that regard. I had a major problem with him continuing to sleep in that bed, though, because for one it was confusing to Lorena and sent a message that there might be hope for reconciliation and more importantly, it put Wayne in an extremely vulnerable position.

I was genuinely concerned for Wayne's safety. I was worried that she might kill him in his sleep or slip some poison into his beloved wine bottle. Wayne did not think she was capable of such violence but since he also had not thought her capable of faking a fatal illness, I wasn't exactly reassured by his opinions about her capacity for certain behaviors.

I expressed my concerns to Wayne and asked him to please at least move to another room while he figured out the living situation. Luckily he humored me by starting to sleep in his son's room since Sebastian didn't sleep in there anyway. The change was tough on Wayne but it was also necessary. Since Wayne has allergies and Sebastian would allow the cat onto his bed during the day, Wayne struggled with having to change the sheets or remove the cat hair before going to bed each night. He was uncomfortable, but at least he was somewhat safer even though I still felt like he was in danger. According to Wayne, even his own mother shared my fears about Lorena being a real danger to him.

The discomfort was a good motivator for Wayne, though, because he started looking for a place to rent temporarily to ride out some of the drama and figure out which direction to take next. I wanted Wayne to move in with me but he wasn't ready and didn't want it to seem like a hasty decision, particularly since nobody knew how long we had really been dating.

# CHAPTER 9: OBSTACLE COURSE

As he searched for the right place to ride out the divorce storm that was brewing, Wayne had a talk with his son about the situation and impending divorce. Sebastian was not entirely surprised by the news. He had noticed that his mom had been spending more time at the house and that her and Wayne had been interacting more than usual, which was a huge red flag for him since his parents rarely interacted prior to the separation. Sebastian was understandably frazzled by the news and immediately messaged his mom about it. The drama hit a high point that night.

When Lorena learned that Wayne had told Sebastian about the divorce, it really set her off. I suppose that made it more real for her and she simply could not handle it so she started calling and messaging Wayne in a frantic emotional state. Wayne knew that it was only going to go downhill from there so he made plans to stay at my house for the night and was luckily able to leave his house before Lorena got there. Wayne and I were both paranoid that night. Lorena had already managed to track down my name and number so we assumed that she also knew where I lived, especially since she had threatened to come to my house if he refused to talk to her.

Wayne and I were on high alert all night, looking out the window and checking the security cameras constantly. We even left Wayne's car at my parent's house instead of in my driveway just to throw her off if she happened to come looking for him. Fortunately Lorena never showed up but that did not stop her from calling and text messaging him like a madwoman for hours on end. It was nice to have Wayne there with me but needless to say, neither of us slept very peacefully that night.

Wayne spent several weeks searching for someplace to rent temporarily. Most options were either too expensive or seemed to be situated in a place just as dramatic as his house had become. Finally after multiple failed viewings, Wayne finally found a decent but tiny efficiency for rent in his area. The place was pricey, but it was clean, quiet, and close to his job. He wasn't planning to stay long and there wasn't much room to work with anyway so Wayne only furnished the efficiency with a futon bed and dubbed the place his bunker.

The next few months were particularly rough on Wayne as he lacked any sense of real stability. Each week, Wayne would bounce back and forth like a ping-pong ball between my house and his bunker. He would go to his house or to his parents' house to visit with his son and parents about three times a week after work and on those nights he would sleep in his bunker. The other nights he would come to my house after work and stay over. It was hard for him on so many levels. In addition to the excessive driving through the hellish traffic as he trekked back and forth between his area and mine on different days, Wayne was essentially torn between two worlds. His parents and son knew about me, but none of them were ready or willing to meet me at that point so Wayne had no choice but to keep his relationship with me separate from his relationship with them. I could see the emotional toll it was taking on him and was frustrated that I couldn't do anything to help. All I could do was remind Wayne that it was only temporary and that it was important for his parents and son to have some time to process the idea of me before actually meeting me.

I understood even then how strange and confusing the whole thing must have been for all of them, particularly because Lorena was doing her best to manipulate their feelings about it and none of them knew the truth about what the real situation was between Wayne and me. Lorena had told Wayne's parents that I was a drug-addicted lesbian with five kids so I couldn't exactly blame them for not jumping at the opportunity to meet me when Wayne kept suggesting it. It certainly was not the type of first impression I wanted the parents of the man I love to have of me, but all I could do was be patient and trust that in time they would see how much Wayne and I love each other and how well we complement each other.

Despite the stress he was under from all of the back and forth, Wayne managed to process it all productively by taking slow but methodical steps to move forward with his divorce and with our relationship. He never allowed the stress or drama to interfere with our relationship and I never did either. No matter what kind of craziness was going on in our worlds with our exes and our families, our love and commitment to each other was always a constant and a safe place to hide from the chaos beyond. The closer Wayne and I got to each other despite being up to our necks in drama, the more convinced I was that our relationship was the real deal after all. I never doubted our love for each other, but I did doubt the possibility of that love escaping all of the drama unscathed because it seemed unlikely to think it was powerful enough to overcome it. My own common sense would not accept it and all of the research I had done about couples that are unfaithful to their spouses and then begin anew with the object of their infidelity only served to perpetuate my fears about our relationship being doomed from the start. But every day as the bond between Wayne and me continued to strengthen, my faith in the durability of our love deepened right along with it.

Slowly but surely, things began to fall into place. Wayne's parents finally agreed to meet me. They agreed to it because they realized how important it was to Wayne, but they certainly still had reservations about it. Wayne made arrangements for him and I to meet his parents and sister for lunch. To say I was nervous about it would be a tremendous understatement. I was aware of the things they had heard about me from Lorena and even though Wayne had obviously made the necessary corrections to those details, there was no doubt that I was coming into this meeting at a huge disadvantage. They knew my history of being with women and knew that I was the one

Wayne had been cheating on Lorena with so it was hard to imagine that his family would be excited about meeting someone who from their perspective had only brought drama into his life.

Wayne and I got to the restaurant first and sat down at a table to wait for his parents and sister to arrive. I tried hard to fight the sense of dread that flooded my mind with fear of their potential judgment of me or of my relationship with Wayne, but it was of little use. My palms were sweaty, my heart was racing, and my stomach was in knots as I saw Wayne's family approaching our table a few minutes later, but fortunately the discomfort was short-lived. I felt almost instantly at ease with all of them. They had a vibe that was very familiar to me, perhaps because it is so similar to the energy present in my own family.

It was such a relief to realize that Wayne's family is just as loveable as he is and that the trash talking Lorena had done would not taint the potential for me to have a good relationship with his parents or his sister. I was happy to have met them and hopeful that meeting his son would also go well whenever he felt ready to do so, though I knew that one was bound to be a bit trickier given his age and circumstances.

Shortly after meeting Wayne's family, the final hearing for my divorce was officially set. I was grateful that my divorce had moved along so smoothly. Aside from some emotional appeals from Janet who thought I was rushing things too quickly and some minor compromises that we had to make on our settlement agreement along the way, the process itself had been relatively painless. Janet made it clear that she was unhappy with the divorce but I tried to be consistent in reminding her that eventually she would come to see that it was the best thing for us all. Though she did not agree or approve, she was cooperative throughout the process so I really can't complain.

Seeing how dramatic and difficult Lorena was making their divorce made me appreciate the fact that Janet was handling our divorce far more maturely, even at its most dramatic points. On the day of the final hearing, my lawyer accompanied me to the courtroom where I had to wait my turn before the judge. Fortunately only the person filing for divorce is required to attend the final hearing unless the other party has an objection or would like to be there. I was grateful that Janet decided not to show and instead contacted me that morning with well wishes for the proceedings, which was as awkward as it was thoughtful.

That morning, I testified that my marriage to Janet was irretrievably broken and that we had amicably reached a settlement agreement concerning property and custody of our daughter. Once I had the final judgment of divorce in my hands, it felt like a tremendous burden had been lifted. The hard part for me was officially over. I still cared about Janet and always will, but breaking those legal ties between us was such a relief. Janet will always be a part of my life as we work together to co-parent in the best way we know how, but putting an official end to our romantic entanglements gave me a much needed sense of freedom. Janet is not a bad person, but she was certainly bad for my self-esteem so the finalization of our divorce was a sign that brighter days were ahead of me.

Janet and I initially agreed to try to maintain some type of "friendship" after the divorce, but this proved to be much more challenging in practice than it had seemed in theory. Lea's birthday was a few weeks after the divorce was finalized and the plan was for all of us to celebrate it together despite the divorce. In an effort to keep things neutral, Janet and I decided to plan a party for Lea at an indoor playground and to split the costs of the festivities.

Things started to get a bit tense between us when I let Janet know that Wayne would be on the guest list for the party, which she understandably objected to. I explained to her, however, that Wayne is my better half and plays a role in our daughter's life too so his attendance at her party was, in my mind, non-negotiable. Needless to say, this caused some friction between Janet and me. I asked her nicely to please try to put her feelings about it aside for our daughter's sake and just be civil. I also argued that it was in her best interest to meet Wayne. After all, he was going to be in Lea's life whether she liked it or not so she should at least meet him and see that he is not the monster she might have imagined.

Janet and men never mixed, but I was hoping that if she met Wayne, she might see that he actually is a good guy who poses no threat to our daughter. Janet thought I was being selfish by inviting him. Wayne told me that he was okay with being left out of the guest list just to keep the peace, but I did not want to compromise on that because I needed Janet to understand and accept that Wayne was not some passing phase. I knew that by insisting Wayne attend the party, it would send a message to Janet that I am serious about my relationship with him and that she could not reasonably expect me to leave him out of social situations just to keep her in her comfort zone. Janet assumed that Wayne was just a plaything for me and that I would soon tire of his masculinity "tainting" my lesbian world. I am sure that Janet was not the only one in my life who harbored these assumptions either. Had Wayne been any other man, they likely would have been right, but because he is who he is, they could not have been more wrong.

The party was admittedly awkward for everyone in attendance. I was grateful for the two-hour time limit that the venue imposed because even one minute longer might have resulted in a dramatic explosion of epic proportions. I recognized the challenge that the situation presented for Janet. She was in a room full of family and friends who were now bearing witness to our "broken" family as my new boyfriend joined the ranks. Even though Wayne and I made it a point to refrain from any PDA and practically stayed on opposite ends of the room from each other nearly the entire time just to make things more comfortable for everyone, seeing him there was understandably hard on Janet. She handled it well enough in that she and her mom both greeted Wayne politely and did not cause a scene about it, but Janet was exuding a negative energy that could be easily felt by anyone within her immediate vicinity and made everybody visibly uncomfortable. Our daughter was no exception to this so Lea unfortunately spent the better part of her party in tears, which broke my heart and made me vow to celebrate her birthday separately from that point forward.

Once the party was over and we were loading Lea's gifts into the car, Janet couldn't hold it in any longer and went off on a handful of my friends in the parking lot about how wrong I had been for bringing Wayne to the party. In her mind, I was doing my daughter a disservice because she expected that I would soon drop Wayne and hurt Lea in the process by letting her get to know Wayne and grow attached to him. Janet could not bring herself to accept that my relationship with Wayne was the real deal. The party's end brought a great deal of relief to everyone that day. It also made me realize that being able to establish a genuine and healthy friendship with Janet was less realistic than I had originally anticipated.

A couple of weeks after Lea's super awkward, third birthday party, Wayne's son decided that he was finally ready to meet me. We planned an outing for the three of us to go to the shooting range and take some shots with my gun. Sebastian obviously felt just as awkward about it as I did, if not more. Conversation between us was forced and somewhat tense, but the weapons safety class and then the shooting helped to break the ice and give us something to talk about. We went to lunch after the range and then took Sebastian home. My meeting him had gone okay but it was clearly going to take some time before the two of us felt comfortable around each other. My daughter was young enough that she freely accepted Wayne upon their first meeting but Sebastian was a pre-teen, which obviously made things much more challenging both for him and for me.

# CHAPTER 10: BLENDING FAMILIES

When Mother's Day rolled around that year, Wayne and I decided that it was the perfect opportunity for our families to meet each other so we planned to get everyone together for an afternoon on the beach. Wayne and I suspected that our parents would get along because they seemed to share a lot of similarities, but I never expected that they would bond as quickly or as easily as they did.

We spent that beautiful, sunny afternoon on the beach celebrating our moms and watching happily as our families started to blend so successfully. Sebastian couldn't be there with us since he was with his mother that day but my daughter, parents, sister, and brother-in-law were all there and connecting naturally with Wayne's parents, sister, and sister's boyfriend's family. My dad learned part of Wayne and my truth that day. He overheard Wayne and I talking about something that had happened a year earlier, which my perceptive father immediately picked up on since according to the story we had told our parents, Wayne and I had allegedly only known each other for a few months at that time.

My dad was hurt that I hadn't been honest with him about the length of my relationship with Wayne, but also relieved to know that it was not actually moving along as hastily as it seemed to those who weren't privy to the true timetable. So my parents learned that Wayne and I had been dating much longer than they thought. They weren't happy about the infidelity obviously, but they were happy that both of us found each other's light while stuck in our respective tunnels of darkness with people who were not well suited for us. They were even happier that our families were just as compatible as Wayne and me. It seemed like the universe had conspired to bring us all together and we were so grateful for that. It was like we all instantly became one big happy family that day. In fact, we were all having such a great time that I completely lost track of time and ended up being about an hour late in getting my daughter back to Janet for her to spend Mother's Day time with her as well. As you might imagine, Janet did not take kindly to my tardiness so that sparked a bit of drama, but now we have agreed to alternate Mother's Day celebrations rather than split them on the same day.

Not long after Sebastian and I had started getting to know each other, Wayne gave up his bunker and moved in with me. There was an extra room in the house so we decided to paint it in Sebastian's favorite colors and make it his so that he could start spending more time with us there. The first several months of blending our little family felt a lot like being on an emotional roller coaster. Lea and Sebastian seemed to instantly take on the role of little sister and big brother by regularly annoying each other along with Wayne and me in the process. They seemed to have and still enjoy a sort of love-hate relationship with each other.

Sebastian and I had our fair share of struggles in the beginning. There were days when I felt sorry for him and what he was going through, days when I genuinely enjoyed spending time with him, and days when I felt like throwing him out of a moving car window. I recall sitting Sebastian down and explaining to him that no matter how we felt about each other, the important thing is that we both love his father and need to learn how to get along, if only for his sake.

It didn't happen overnight. There was a lot of resistance on both sides, but with a great deal of patience and persistence, Sebastian and I were finally able to establish a healthy friendship that continues to grow daily. I had always felt like I was destined to adopt a troubled teen and while it certainly wasn't the situation I had originally envisioned, Sebastian came into my world and made that dream come true. They say to be careful what you wish for and this was no exception because there were days when I wondered if we could ever make it work but in the end, I am so grateful to be a part of Sebastian's life and have grown to love him as unconditionally as I love his father.

It is such a blessing that our families get along as beautifully as they do. Wayne and I are both highly family oriented so it was crucial that our families connect, but neither of us ever dreamt that they would click quite as much as they do. Our children, our parents, our siblings, and even our cousins all love each other and genuinely enjoy spending time together, which can often be such a rare thing in families bound by marriage rather than by blood. Our family blended seamlessly on every level and I could not be more grateful for the bond we all share.

# CHAPTER 11: CLOSING CHAPTERS

Two months after Wayne and I started living together, Janet took Lea on vacation for a week. I got to speak to Lea every night before bed as is our custom, but on one particular night, it was nearing midnight and I still hadn't heard from Lea. I messaged Janet asking her to have Lea call me so that I could go to sleep, but she did not respond nor did she answer when I called. I was beginning to worry so I called and messaged a few more times, but was unable to get through. By the time Janet finally had Lea call just after midnight, my patience had worn thin and disappeared altogether when all I heard on the other end was Lea crying hysterically. Frustrated and angry, I hung up the phone. A few minutes later, Janet called to explain that Lea was crying because she did not want to return to the room.

It became immediately apparent to me that Janet was heavily intoxicated. I knew she wasn't driving because the two of them were staying in an all-inclusive resort, but that did not alleviate my concern or my anger over Janet's irresponsible decision to drink so heavily while knowing that she was the only adult responsible for Lea's welfare at the time. Janet called me repeatedly babbling and slurring nonsense while Lea continued to cry in the background. I was worried and furious, but Janet kept going on and on about how she realized that I am in love with Wayne and how much it hurt her to see me so in love with somebody else. The alcohol had completely shut down

Janet's filter and she was laying into me with all of the anger, hurt, and resentment that she had been bottling up since our separation.

I sat there on the other end of the line listening to Janet and debating whether or not I should get dressed and make the four-hour drive to the resort to ensure my daughter's safety, but relaxed once they got back to the room and Lea seemed to settle down and fall asleep. Janet and I spent about two hours on the phone that night going back and forth between crying and fighting. I was furious that she had gotten so drunk while caring for our daughter, but also cognizant of the fact that this kind of behavior was definitely out of character for her. Something she said made me realize what had triggered the whole incident. Apparently Janet had seen something I posted on social media about Wayne and despite our already being divorced, the realization of what I felt for Wayne overwhelmed her in ways she wasn't expecting so she drank more than she should have to compensate.

That night was the most challenging for me since the initial separation. It hurt to hear Janet in so much pain and know that I was the cause of it, but I was still confident that I had made the best possible decision for all of us even if Janet wasn't ready to accept it at the time. As angry as I was for her putting our daughter's safety in jeopardy, I trusted that Janet would not repeat that mistake again so I forgave her for her poor judgment but knew deep down that the landscape of my relationship with her had been permanently altered. It was clear to me then that trying to remain "friends" with Janet was only going to do more damage and increase the potential of a bigger falling out between us down the road. I made up my mind then that any future interactions between Janet and me would be strictly limited to issues related to our daughter. Friendship was simply not going to work so a cordial co-parenting relationship would have to be as good as it gets between us. That was a difficult decision for me to make because I do care about Janet and valued the friendship that we shared in the past, but I knew that it was necessary in order to preserve our respect for each other and keep the resentment to a minimum. Janet was angry when I told her that I didn't think we should be friends but again, I only did what I thought was best for us both.

As things started to finally settle down on my end, Wayne was starting to near the end of the finish line on his own divorce. Lorena kept trying to delay the paperwork as much as she could, but Wayne wasn't falling for her games anymore. At one point, Lorena even tried to drag me into it when Wayne wasn't budging on a deadline to return a signed document. She caught me by surprise by calling me from a number that I didn't recognize and then asking me to convince Wayne to give her more time. Of course she had a slew of excuses for why she needed extra time and presented them to me rather skillfully, proving to be a master manipulator because despite knowing her reputation for deceit, I was almost convinced that she was sincere. Luckily Lorena eventually started to accept that her hopes for reunification with Wayne were a lost cause. Once she finally accepted that Wayne and I were serious about each other and that she would never win him back, she set her sights on a new target and was eager to move the divorce along so that she could lock in her next victim. Four months after my own divorce was finalized, Wayne finally had a date for his divorce's final judgment. It was set for a couple of weeks before his birthday so it certainly made for an excellent early birthday present.

Wayne was so excited about his impending divorce that he started to talk about us getting married, which kind of threw me for a loop. Up until that point, I hadn't given much thought to the idea of getting remarried. In fact, I think I kind of assumed that neither of us would want to get married again considering how poorly marriage had treated us in the past. It wasn't that I didn't think our relationship would last. On the contrary, I was confident that our relationship was built to last even without the legal ties of marriage. Besides marriage had left such a bad taste in both of our mouths that I was genuinely shocked to know he was even considering going there again with me.

I had no doubt that I wanted to be with Wayne for the rest of my life, but I was scared that marriage might hinder rather than help our relationship. That fear took over as I told Wayne that it was too soon to be talking about marriage, especially since he wasn't even officially divorced yet. I imagined him picking up his final divorce decree and then the two of us going to another floor of the courthouse to apply for a marriage license, but this notion was not exactly appealing to me. If we were going to get married, I did not want it to be immediately after our divorces. We had only been living together for a few months and still needed time to get our groove going before taking such a big leap forward. I could tell that Wayne was disappointed by my reaction to his suggestion, but I simply wasn't ready to consider marriage again at that time.

# CHAPTER 12: NEW BEGINNINGS

Once Wayne's divorce was finalized, we went out to celebrate with his parents, sister, and Sebastian. It was crazy to think of how far we had both come in a relatively short period of time. Within the span of seven months, Wayne and I had finalized two divorces and created a brand new family with each other. Had someone told me what was to come on the day I first met Wayne, I never would have believed it. Somehow we had made the impossible possible and successfully navigated our relationship through tidal waves of emotional debris and into the safe harbor surrounding the little slice of paradise that we carved out for ourselves.

At long last Wayne and I were basking in calm waters together. I couldn't help but wonder if that would be the death of us. Perhaps our relationship thrived on the drama and might be compromised by the serenity of our newfound peace. After all, there was nothing but suspense and uncertainty up to that point so it made sense to think that not having it anymore might pose a problem of its own.

Would we get bored of each other if things were too simple? Would we long for the rush of the secrecy under which we fell in love? Fortunately the answer to those questions was a quick and resounding "no." The peace and quiet coursed happily through our relationship, weaving our lives together seamlessly and strengthening the roots of our love as they propelled even deeper into the fabric of forever.

Wayne and I both learned so much from the pain of our past and those lessons have been critical in helping us to make better decisions in our present as we strive to produce a brighter future for us both and for our families.

After a few months of steadily increasing happiness and intimacy, it became apparent to me that I had been foolish to think the peace might be detrimental. Neither of us missed the drama one bit. We relished the ease with which our love continued to evolve and developed an unwavering confidence that together we can overcome any obstacle life might throw at us. I realized that my attitude towards love and marriage had been completely redefined. Wayne and the love I shared with him effortlessly reshaped my perception of marriage's value and led me to the conclusion that nothing would make me happier than to marry my best friend and soul mate.

Wayne and I were in the middle of a romantic trip to a tropical island when I knew beyond the shadow of a doubt that I wanted to experience what a loving and healthy marriage was like and that there was nobody I could do that better with than Wayne. Marriage no longer felt like a bad word to me. Instead it represented love, hope, and all that is beautiful in the world. Since I had already tabled the discussion with Wayne, though, I knew that he was going to wait a while before bringing the idea of marriage up again. I wanted him to know that I was ready and happily eager to marry him, but I wanted to make it special by planning a proposal for him. I know that tradition says the man should do the asking but considering there was nothing traditional about our relationship, I thought it was only fitting that I flip the script on proposing too.

I spent a few weeks conducting research for ideas on how a woman might propose to her man and really liked the idea of a scavenger hunt, but had a hard time deciding on how to best present the final step. I wasn't sure if the clues should lead to a tangible object like a ring or some other gift for him or if they should simply lead to the big question on its own. I was leaning towards popping the question as the final clue but was still stumped on what medium to use for that. I definitely wanted music to play a role in the proposal so I knew I had to find the perfect song to complement my feelings about him and about marrying him.

After much searching, I found exactly what I was looking for in a song by Sara Bareilles called "I Choose You," which was spot on in saying precisely what I felt. Wayne typically has a hard time processing the lyrics in music so I printed out the words for him to read while listening to it. I loved the song and was certain that it would play a role in my proposal, but still felt like something was missing.

Eventually the missing piece shot into my mind like a bolt of lightning: the perfect way to propose to Wayne was to lead him right back to where it all began on Craigslist. I immediately got to work on drafting my clues and the text for my final Craigslist proposal ad. There were a total of four clues, each one hidden within a memento from our relationship decorating our home and the last one leading him to the Casual Encounters section of Craigslist where there was a post titled "--- (Initials) Stole My Heart Instead of My Liver." The post included the following graphic and text:

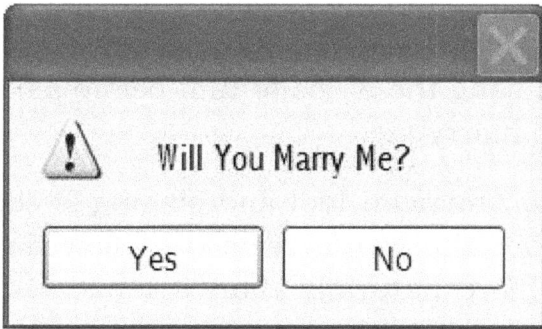

*'I didn't fall in love with you. I walked into love with you, with my eyes wide open, choosing to take every step along the way. I do believe in fate and destiny, but I also believe that we are only fated to do the things we would choose anyway. And I'd choose you; in a hundred lifetimes, in a hundred different worlds, in any version of reality, I'd find you and I'd choose you.'* (Kiersten White, The Chaos of Stars)

*"Thanks to you and your love, my heart has blossomed in ways I never imagined possible. Walking into this love with you was the best decision I have ever made and I want nothing more than to keep on walking right along side you for the rest of our days.*

*WILL YOU MARRY ME?"*

Once everything was ready for the proposal, I planned a romantic weekend getaway to celebrate our "Freedom Flight" anniversary. The idea was to hand Wayne the first clue to his scavenger hunt the moment we got home that weekend, but the passion and intimacy we shared during that staycation led me to spill the beans earlier than I had anticipated. In the midst of a passionate moment during our trip, I spontaneously played the Sara Bareilles song on my phone and sang the lyrics to him before asking Wayne if he would marry me.

I am no American Idol and singing is certainly not my forte, but the words seemed to flow directly from my heart more naturally than if I had written them myself. The lyrics to the song read:

*"Let the bough break, let it come down crashing*
*Let the sun fade out to a dark sky*
*I can't say I'd even notice it was absent*
*'Cause I could live by the light in your eyes*
*I'll unfold before you*
*Would have strung together*
*The very first words of a lifelong love letter*


*Tell the world that we finally got it all right*
*I choose*
*You*
*I will become yours and you will become mine*
*I choose*
*You*
*I choose*
*You, yeah*

*There was a time when I would have believed them*
*If they told me that you could not come true*
*Just love's illusion*
*But then you found me*
*And everything changed*
*And I believe in something again*

*My whole heart*
*Will be yours forever*
*This is a beautiful start*
*To a lifelong love letter*

*Tell the word that we finally got it all right*
*I choose*
*You*
*I will become yours and you will become mine*
*I choose*
*You*
*I choose*
*You*

*We are not perfect we'll learn from our mistakes*
*And as long as it takes I will prove my love to you*
*I am not scared of the elements I am underprepared,*
*But I am willing*
*And even better*
*I get to be the other half of you*

*Tell the world that we finally got it all right*
*I choose*
*You, yeah*

*I will become yours and you will become mine*
*I choose*
*You*
*I choose*
*You*

*I choose*
*You"*


Wayne was shocked and confused at first, but once he realized that I was serious, he said "yes" and we cried happy tears while holding each other tight. I told him about my original plan and the scavenger hunt that was waiting for him at home. Then I pulled up the Craigslist ad for him to read. Wayne was speechless for a little while and then expressed how happy he was that I had changed my mind. He also wanted to know what it was that had made me change my mind.

I explained to Wayne that I married Janet out of a sense of obligation. Essentially I allowed her to pressure me into marriage and had made that commitment to her for all of the wrong reasons. But when I thought about marrying Wayne, there was no sense of obligation whatsoever, only joy at the thought of getting to be the other half of him. The more I thought about it, the more I realized that if I married Janet for all of the wrong reasons, I would be crazy to not marry Wayne for all of the right ones. It wasn't about having to get married, it was about genuinely wanting to get married because I have never loved anyone like I love him and there is nobody in the universe that I would rather spend the rest of my life with than Wayne.

Janet and I legally married by getting the marriage license and having a friend notarize it over drinks at a local restaurant. We took few pictures, but I did not share any of them on social media or elsewhere. I was not proud or excited about the marriage in any way and just wanted to get it over with and hope that it might miraculously solve all of the problems we had. It didn't take long to figure out that marrying her was a huge mistake and that our problems would only continue to worsen in its wake. My upcoming marriage to Wayne was noticeably different on all levels. I was so excited to marry him and wanted the world to know how happy I was to be blessed with such an incredible partner in life. We originally planned to wed six months after our engagement, but after a month or so of planning, we decided to move it up a few months sooner because it held the promise of better weather for our dream outdoor wedding and also because I could not wait to be married to him.

Wayne and I shared the same vision for our wedding day. We both wanted to spend quality time with our loved ones in a relaxed, waterside environment where we would exchange vows and make a lifetime commitment to one another. It was important to both of us to keep things simple and casual. Initially as we searched for the perfect venue, we were exploring a variety of beachfront hotels and also considering taking to the waters by having our ceremony on a boat of some kind. As beautiful as most of those venues were, none of them felt right to us. We were not impressed with the formality of it all, which we were hoping to get away from.

The idea of being held to a strict timeline of events or of having to dress too formally was not appealing to either one of us. Plus none of the event coordinators at any of the venues we visited seemed to be on board with our non-negotiable desire to jump into the water together immediately following the ceremony. In fact, most of them seemed quite confused as to why we would want to do such a thing. We realized that it was not exactly conventional, but from the moment we decided to get married, jumping into the water together was something that both of us truly wanted as part of our ceremony. We wanted to take the plunge as literally as we were figuratively and we were not willing to cut that out of our plans. Some of the venues were willing to humor us in that regard, but it was obvious they did not agree with it.

Ultimately, Wayne and I decided that we were not going to use any venue that required a wedding coordinator. We wanted to coordinate our own wedding so that there was no pressure on us or anybody else to do things in a certain way or in a pre-determined order. Our wedding was supposed to be a celebration of our love and since we are fortunate enough for that love to flow freely and organically, it was important to us that our wedding day be representative of that.

I suggested to Wayne that instead of searching for a new venue, we could create our own by renting a waterfront home from Airbnb and using it to host our dream wedding in the back yard. Wayne loved the idea so I got to work on searching for the perfect house to rent. The house search turned out to be quite a process. Most of the homes available for rent on Airbnb that met our criteria were priced beyond our ideal budget preferences, had strict restrictions about using the property to host social events, or were not available for our desired date range. The plan was to rent a place with a waterfront yard that was suitable for a casual wedding and where we could relax for a long weekend with our parents and kids. After a few weeks of searches and futile inquiries, the perfect beach house came up and we were able to book it from Friday to Monday of our wedding weekend. The house was ideal in every way. The price was just right, there was enough space for our entire family to stay comfortably, and the owner gave us permission to host a small wedding in the beautiful, waterfront back yard.

In the weeks leading to our wedding weekend, my mom and future mother-in-law were stressing out over my and Wayne's casual approach to wedding planning. We had already done the hardest part, which was securing the right location, so we were pretty relaxed about all the other little details. It was important to us that our wedding be a stress-free event for us and for our guests.

Much to Wayne's and everyone else's surprise, I decided that I would wear a wedding dress for the actual ceremony. Dressing up and more specifically, wearing an actual dress, is not exactly a commonplace occurrence for me. I am not a fan of makeup, dresses, or anything that is traditionally feminine and wasn't initially planning to go that route for the wedding. Wayne never pressured me to wear anything specific; he suggested that I wear whatever I felt most comfortable with and my mom along with most of my friends assumed that I would likely wear nice pants with a blouse or something along those lines. That is one of the things I love most about Wayne: he always encourages me to be myself and loves me unconditionally just the way I am. After looking at some wedding dresses online, though, I started liking the idea of going with a casual and comfortable wedding dress. I also liked the idea of getting my hair and makeup professionally done for the event. Marrying Wayne was a momentous occasion for me so it made sense to do something out of the ordinary to commemorate just how special of an event it was.

Dress shopping actually turned out to be much more fun than I had anticipated. I had done considerable research online ahead of time so I knew exactly what I was looking for when I went to a local bridal shop with my mom and a few of my closest friends, all of whom got a serious kick out of watching me try on dresses. Aside from when I was a young kid and had no say in what I wore, dresses were definitely not a part of my wardrobe so the dress shopping was a welcome treat for those who joined me. Three was the magic number as the third dress that I tried on turned out to be exactly what I was looking for. The price was right, which was extremely important since I planned on taking this dress for a swim so spending a fortune on it was not an option. I wish I had captured the face of the bridal worker who helped me after I told her that

I planned to jump into the pool with the dress on. She thought I was kidding at first and then likely assumed I was nuts when she realized how serious I was.

The dress was light, comfortable, and not too formal, which made it really easy to say "yes to the dress" immediately after trying it on. I had fun with my people and enjoyed a happy hour celebration at the bar next to the bridal shop once we were done. Wayne kept his wedding attire simple as well. He wanted to wear something nice but casual since my dress was somewhat casual and we were having an outdoor wedding with plans to jump into the pool fully clothed. Wayne ultimately decided on wearing dark jeans with a white button down shirt and khaki vest. We were both set on changing into more comfortable clothing as soon as we finished taking our plunge so we made sure to let our guests know that casual attire was preferred and that they should also bring a bathing suit (something I'm sure is a rarity on most wedding invites).

Our wedding day could not have been more magical or spectacular than it turned out to be. We kept our guest list small with only immediate family and a handful of close friends in attendance. Since we wanted to enjoy the whole day with each other and those we love, we planned a poolside brunch wedding. Wayne made our wedding arch from scratch and it turned out more beautiful than any of the ones we were looking at renting. We hired a catering team to prepare and serve a delicious brunch and a photographer to capture all of the special moments.

My aunt and mom provided lovely flower arrangements that brought the place to life and I set up a fun photo booth with a bunch of props to take silly pictures. My sister-in-law created a special wedding soundtrack for the festivities including our wedding song, "All of Me Loves All of You" by John Legend and of course the Sara Bareilles song that I had sung to him during the proposal along with several other favorite tunes.

We chose not to have a wedding party but my daughter and Wayne's son both served as our ring bearers, my father officiated the ceremony, and my good friend notarized our marriage license. The whole day was intimate, casual, and bursting with love and good vibes.

Since we were planning to jump into the pool immediately following the ceremony, I asked the photographer to take as many pictures as possible before we began the ceremony since the hair, makeup, and dress were going to be subjected to ice cold, chlorine water and would therefore likely be much less photogenic afterwards.

Just before 11 am, Wayne and I were dressed and ready for our close ups. We took a series of photographs with each other, with our kids, our families, our friends, and even a few photo booth props too. Once we were done with the pictures, Wayne and I stood under the homemade arch that we placed near the pool. My father read from the original script that I had provided for him, but also added a beautiful speech of his own in the process. Wayne and I exchanged personal vows and then sealed them with our rings and a kiss. The ceremony was brief but brimming with love and emotion. Wayne and I tried to hold back the tears as we exchanged our vows, but it was impossible for us both (though I was more successful at controlling it for fear that I'd ruin my makeup before even jumping into the pool). That moment and the entire day was literally a dream come true for both of us. Somehow that tall, handsome stranger in the Starbucks shop was now officially my loving husband and better half. I am still not sure how I got so ridiculously lucky, but I am grateful for him and his love every single moment of every day that we are so blessed to share together.

As soon as the ceremony was finished, Wayne and I grabbed each other's hands and prepared to leap into the pool. Family and friends were torn on the idea. Some of them cheered us on while many begged us not to do it since we both looked so nice and they didn't want to see all that effort get ruined. Wayne and I were apprehensive more than anything because despite being a beautiful and warm, sunny day, the pool had no heater and the water temperature was far colder than either of us were comfortable with, but taking the plunge literally was something we were both set on doing.

Wayne and I looked into each other's eyes and agreed to go forward with our plan to take the leap. On the count of three, Wayne and I jumped up and into the freezing pool. The bottom of my dress came up and over my head as my feet touched the bottom of the pool. Wayne and I shot up from the cold surface, screaming and laughing as we bee-lined our way to the steps of the pool where our mothers were waiting for us with towels. We were shivering from the cold dunk, but the adrenaline was pumping and we were so happy to have taken the plunge together in every possible way.

Wayne and I dried off a bit and then ran inside to take a quick shower and change into drier, more comfortable clothes. Somehow my hair and makeup remained mostly intact even after the pool jump and the shower. Apparently it pays to tell your stylist that you plan to jump in the pool so she gives your look the fortitude to withstand your crazy ideas. Wayne and I came out after our shower in casual, comfortable threads and joined the party for brunch and bottomless mimosas.

The sun was shining, the music was jamming, drinks were flowing, and everywhere we looked there were people we loved. We literally could not have asked for anything better. Shortly after brunch, our guests started changing into their bathing suits. We laid towels and blankets out on the lawn, turned on the karaoke, and spent hours enjoying an impromptu grassy gathering with the people we love most. We sang together, took lots of pictures, snacked on goodies, drank to our hearts' content, and took turns jumping into the canal behind the house.

The most memorable thing about our wedding day was the sheer volume of pure love. Our families and friends blend together as beautifully as Wayne and me so it was remarkable to see everyone truly enjoying themselves and each other. The love flowing between everyone present was literally palpable; a truly magical experience that only served to further validate how Wayne and me were undoubtedly destined to be together. All of our friends and family in attendance raved about how much fun they had at our wedding, which is exactly what we envisioned for our perfect day.

There was no rush to do certain things in specific order or that formal, stuffy feeling that Wayne and I hate about the average wedding. From the moment it began until late into that night, our wedding was intimate, casual, and loads of fun for everyone involved. No stress, no drama; only love and the making of happy memories to last a lifetime.

I am so grateful to have married Wayne and for the incredible family that my family and I inherited along with him. Our love was written into the fabric of fate long before our paths ever crossed, but now that they have finally intersected, there is no greater joy in the entire world than to share this journey together.

# CHAPTER 13: THE TAKEAWAY

During my time on this Earth, I have noticed that the most challenging experiences tend to unveil the deepest truths and teach the most powerful lessons. My experience with Wayne is certainly no exception. Despite having suffered through some trying times in our previous relationships, both before and after we came into each other's lives, Wayne and I gained some invaluable gems of insight along the way.

My divorce and the road that led to it taught me so much about what it takes to have a happy and successful marriage, the fruits of which I am fortunate enough to share now with Wayne. My first marriage did not crumble overnight, but it wasn't until I was sifting through the ruins that I discovered the wealth of secrets buried deep beneath the rubble. Those pearls of wisdom may have come too late to save my first marriage, but they arrived just in time to pave a solid foundation for my last one and I will share them here in the hopes that they continue to help others who may be facing similar struggles.

**RESPECT.** Respect for myself and for my partner is of utmost importance for a successful relationship. The most destructive force in my first marriage was a lack of respect. While Janet did behave disrespectfully towards me in a multitude of ways over the years, I blame myself more than I do her. It wasn't right for Janet to treat me the way that she did, but it was my fault for allowing her to continually disrespect me without consequence. I made excuses for her behavior and rarely stood up for myself when she would do or say things that belittled or humiliated me. If I had had more respect for myself, I would not have tolerated that sort of treatment, but it took my leaving the situation to finally be able to see that clearly. I learned that having self-respect and respect for my partner are crucial cornerstones for a healthy and happy relationship.

Wayne and I both understand the value of respect and are committed to maintaining it within our relationship. We don't always agree with each other, but we do always respect each other's right to disagree. We value each other's opinions and idiosyncrasies, even when they don't necessarily jive with our own. Mutual respect is a non-negotiable component of a healthy and happy relationship. Without respect, you might as well call it quits because it will never work long term. Also, it is far easier to maintain respect than it is to regain it. Once respect has been lost, getting it back is an awfully slippery slope so your efforts would be better invested in trying not to lose it in the first place.

Do not allow anger or frustration to make you say things you may later regret. If you feel yourself getting heated to that point, ask your partner to give you a few minutes to cool down before you resume your discussion of the issue at hand. It's too easy to fall into a pattern of disrespecting each other by saying mean or insulting things out of anger. Give yourself and your partner space and time during challenging arguments so that you can work it out thoughtfully and respectfully.

**HONESTY.** Honesty is the number one rule in my marriage with Wayne. It has been that way from the moment he and I decided to pursue a relationship both in secret and beyond the veil. We were not honest with our spouses at the time, but we understood that this was part of the reason why we found ourselves in the predicament we were in to begin with.

It's not always easy to be honest. It sounds simple enough in theory, but things tend to get a little tricky when it's time to be honest about issues that may lead to hurt feelings or unpleasant confrontations. Being dishonest sometimes means telling blatant lies, but more often than not the dishonesty comes in less obvious forms like sugarcoating truths or omitting facts altogether.

The lack of honesty in my first marriage looked like sugarcoating my level of unhappiness when discussing it with my wife or sweeping my feelings under the rug one too many times until the heap beneath the floor made it impossible for either of us to stand steadily on it. As I got used to sugarcoating things or ignoring topics we should have been resolving, my dishonesty evolved into more dangerous territory as I started sneaking around behind Janet's back and looking for secret lovers to fill the void that I couldn't bring myself to address with her.

There were times when I did try. Times when I told Janet directly of my unhappiness and unmet needs; times when I begged her to go to therapy with me or do something to try and fix things between us. No matter how hard I tried, though, Janet always resisted and insisted on continuing to sweep more stuff under the rug until I started being dishonest even with myself by failing to accept just how bad things had gotten between us. In the back of my mind, I knew that it was over, but could not bring myself to admit it or do anything about it. Instead, I continued on my path of increasing dishonesty when what I really should have done was end the relationship once and for all. Wayne and I both understand how critical it is to be honest with each other, even and especially about the things that are most challenging. We recognize that failure to be honest with each other will jeopardize our marriage and after all we went through to get to where we are, that is not a risk that either of us is willing to take. I would much rather be honest with Wayne about the tough stuff and work through it than avoid a momentary discomfort at the expense of our love.

**COMMUNICATION.** Next up is communication, which of course is closely related to both respect and honesty. Like honesty, communication is easiest when things are light and simple, but becomes more challenging when the going gets tough, which happens to be precisely when it counts the most. Respect and honesty are both best conveyed through open lines of communication with a partner.

Wayne and I communicate openly and honestly with each other in a variety of ways. We often express affection and appreciation for one another through words, little notes, touch, and romantic gestures. We also use communication to help resolve disagreements or issues that may arise by talking through our feelings and making an effort to understand where the other is coming from. If one of us has a concern about something, we say so. We check in with each other often to find out if there is anything that we can improve about our relationship or the way we interact with each other. This kind of open and ongoing communication will help us to prevent our relationship from growing stagnant and keep us in tune with our feelings and what we need to continue working successfully as a team.

When we come to a point where talking about certain things becomes too uncomfortable or volatile, as they are destined to do in a long-term relationship, I plan to rely on written communication to help get us through. Writing down feelings in a letter is an excellent way to communicate about tough issues with a partner because it gives both people a chance to process their emotions and think carefully about what they are going to say before they say it, which helps maintain both respect and honesty in even the most challenging of situations. Communicating is not always easy, but it is always well worth the effort.

**ROMANCE.** Last but certainly not least in this list of insights is romance, which is naturally tied to intimacy. While respect, honesty, and communication are all essential components of a happy and healthy relationship, romance is critical because it is the one thing that sets a romantic relationship apart from the rest.

The movies and other media outlets tend to portray romance in generic ways and that sometimes limits people's understanding of what romance actually looks like in the real world. Yes, flowers, chocolate, candle-lit dinners, and long walks on the beach are all lovely ways to stir up some romance with a partner, but there are also countless other paths to romance, many of which are far more meaningful than what is typically depicted on the big screen.

When it comes to romance and deepening intimacy with a partner, the little things tend to mean the most. It's about showing your partner that you care through simple gestures that show thoughtfulness and appreciation. Some of the ways that I do this for Wayne include getting up earlier than I have to sometimes just to make him coffee in the morning before he goes to work or to make sure he doesn't forget his lunch, which I often sneak a note into wishing him a good day and reminding him of how much I love him.

One day not too long ago, I came home from a stressful day at work to find that Wayne had gotten home early to surprise me. He had cooked dinner, greeted me at the door with a kiss and a glass of champagne, and had our bedroom set up for him to give me a massage. When Wayne had to travel for work recently and we made plans for me to join him a day later on the trip, I arrived at the hotel room to find that he had spelled "I love you" out on the bed using peanuts and left other cute little notes throughout the room since he was still going to be at work upon my arrival.

Wayne and I both make a conscious effort to share ongoing, quality alone time together by going out to dinner or sometimes just watching some of our favorite shows. We both value physical affection and frequently hold hands, caress each other, or simply cuddle close together as often as possible, which works wonders for maintaining intimacy.

True romance does not require spending a lot of money or making any elaborate plans. The only thing you need for genuine, meaningful romance is effort. It's about being present in the relationship and making a conscious, daily effort to show your appreciation and love for each other. It might sound simple enough, but the truth is that many couples quickly fail in this area because they get lazy in love and complacent about romance. They often start to take each other for granted and spread their attention thin by focusing more on their smart phones or any other distraction than they do each other.

Wayne and I go out to dinner often and can't help but notice how many couples and families go out together without ever really sharing anything other than space at the table because they spend the majority of their time looking at a screen instead of talking to each other. Romance is about putting the phone down, looking each other in the eyes, and giving your partner the most valuable thing you have: your undivided attention. It's about making an ongoing effort to remind your partner, through words or actions (and preferably both) that you love and appreciate his or her presence in your life.

Another important aspect of romance and intimacy, however, is keeping the passion alive in order to maintain a happy and healthy sex life. If sex is neglected in the romantic arena, all of your other efforts will have been in vain. Some people might try to downplay the importance of sex in a relationship, but speaking from personal experience, a breakdown in the bedroom was the trigger that eventually led to a breakdown in every other area of the relationship during my first marriage so I recognize that keeping the passion alive is a critical component of keeping the relationship afloat as well. A healthy sex life requires everything that a healthy relationship does: respect, honesty, communication, and romance.

Wayne and I are lucky. We are highly compatible as both friends and lovers. We genuinely enjoy each other's company, we love each other unconditionally, and we are committed to each other and to our children. Our journey through two divorces and then a new marriage to each other has taught us many things, but one of the most notable lessons gained from this entire process is that our time is too precious to squander on relationships that are made of anything less than genuine love.

Consider for a moment that you have only one day left to live. Who would you want to see on that last day? If the people occupying the biggest space in your life right at this moment would not make that list then it's time to start making some big changes. Whether we like to admit it or not, we all have less time than we think we do, which is why it is so important to invest our precious moments wisely. If you have already found your own Wayne then nurture that love and treat it like the treasure that it is. If you are still searching for your Wayne, keep your hopes high and remember that there is no better GPS than the human heart.

Thank you for reading my story. Now get out there and start writing yours!

## ABOUT THE AUTHOR

Kris Calbar lives with her husband, Wayne, and their little tribe of human and furry creatures. She writes as a hobby and loves her top-secret day job, which takes up most the time she might otherwise spend doing more writing.

www.ingramcontent.com/pod-product-compliance
Lightning Source LLC
Chambersburg PA
CBHW061738020426
42331CB00006B/1282